# Spirit Media's

ULTIMATE
Book Marketing
Guide

Book Promotion Tactics
Guaranteed to Increase Sales

Kevin White, CEO

Spirit Media's ULTIMATE Book Marketing Guide

Book Promotion Tactics
Guaranteed to Increase Sales

Kevin White, CEO

2023© by Kevin White

All rights reserved. Published 2023.

BIBLE SCRIPTURES

Printed in the United States of America

🔥 SPIRIT MEDIA
www.spiritmedia.us
1249 Kildaire Farm Rd STE 112
Cary, NC 27511
1 (888) 800-3744

Books › Business & Money › Marketing & Sales
Industrial Marketing
Market Research Business

Paperback ISBN: 978-1-958304-51-8
Audiobook ISBN: 978-1-958304-53-2
eBook ISBN: 978-1-958304-52-5
Library of Congress Control Number: 2023900356

Register This New Book

Benefits of Registering*

• FREE replacements of lost or damaged books
• FREE audiobook—*Get to the Point* by Kevin White
• FREE information about new titles and other freebies

spiritmedia.us/register

*See our website for requirements and limitations

Money-Back Guarantee

I am so confident this book will absolutely increase your book sales that I am offering you a full money-back guarantee.

If you implement the marketing tactics in this book and do not experience a measurable increase in the sale of your book, simply return your copy of this book for a full refund. No questions asked.

Kevin White

Kevin White, CEO

Acknowledgement

This book represents years of research I've done with the help of my team at Spirit Media®.

Before there was Spirit Media®, it was Ana, Jay, and Justin that helped me turn my own books into international bestsellers. Thank you for entering the test lab with me and helping me prove every tactic in this book.

Thank you, Ana, for investing countless hours of research and for compiling the tactics found in this book.

Thank you, Jay, for being our resident keyword guru.

Thank you, Justin, for helping me put four different postage stamps on hundreds of books in front of the Apex Post Office the day we both tested positive for Covid. Those were fun times.

Thank you, Steve, for helping us write and turn our research into chapters.

Thank you Angela, Jim, and Barbara for allowing us to tell your stories.

Thank you Carol, Carlene, and Marj for editing and proofing the book.

To everyone at Spirit Media®, thank you for turning this book into a reality.

Client Testimonials

"Books change people's lives. Spirit Media® has created something that enables us to get our books and message out to the world. I am very honored and excited to be part of this venture." - BARBARA HEMPHILL

"Spirit Media® helps me with all that nitty gritty marketing that I didn't necessarily want to do. I love my website and having all the help that Spirit Media® provides through their very capable and talented staff."
- CHRISTINE SMITH

"God has raised Spirit Media® up at the right time. I was looking for someone like Spirit Media® to help with a book that I had published and to do some of the marketing. Such a blessing!" - ROGER LOOMIS

"Spirit Media® made a sales pitch and it was over delivered. I have never had a partner that I could completely trust and know that they're going to do exactly what they say they're gonna do. And that is freedom." - MARTIN MEYER

Introduction

Do you have a book . . . that's NOT selling?

You are actually part of a very small, elite group of authors. Why? Because 80% of people would like to write a book, but less than 1% are actively writing and publishing it. If you have a book in process, you're part of that 1% elite.

The fact is—most independent authors' books sell fewer than 250 copies because they've put their book on the market but never effectively marketed.

Let's contrast that with the huge book market. In 2021, $25.93 billion (with a B) worth of books were sold in the U.S., according to zippia.com. From 2019 to 2021, eBook sales alone increased in the United States by over $100 million (from $983.3 million to $1.1 billion), according to statistica.com.

And that's only considering the United States. In Canada, book sales almost doubled during the same period. What about the rest of the world?

Did you know that the U.S. represents only 4% of the total readers in the world? God tells us to share His message with the nations.

There's an enormous growing hunger and demand all over the world for quality book reading material. Your book and your message are needed. This is your opportunity.

But, catching the big wave of writing and selling a book is something like surfing. The best surfers in the world all know that every surfer wanting to take advantage of the next big wave must be ready. Without expert, attentive preparation, surfers call it "guaranteed wipeout".

Most independent authors' books sell fewer than 250 copies because they lack expert preparation. That's an author's "wipeout" nightmare.

For the author, the Spirit Media® ONE platform changes that. We are specialists who effectively help authors take their book from conception to writing to marketing.

Think about it. Reading this book, *Spirit Media's ULTIMATE Guide to Book Marketing*, will be much faster than earning a master's degree in marketing. It's also much more budget friendly and has proven to radically boost book sales for so many authors.

This guide to marketing your book reveals how you (the author) will partner with Spirit Media® to conceive, write, market, and sell your book successfully.

When you systematically execute the process and recommendations laid out here, it can take you to levels you only dreamed of.

By the end of this book you'll see why our customers love Spirit Media®. Welcome to *Spirit Media's ULTIMATE Guide to Book Marketing*.

If you are looking for the right publishing company
that cares for the writer, book, and the reader,
Spirit Media is for you!
- Dr. Temsula Bass

Table of Contents

CHAPTER

Start Marketing While Writing

If you haven't yet published your book . . .

Good news. You can immediately incorporate this chapter BEFORE you publish.

If you have already published your book . . .

Don't worry, this chapter is not going to leave you with tons of regret. If you have already published your book, then it is what it is. It would be a disservice to you to not include this chapter.

It is never too late or too early to consider a book makeover.

The good news is your book is not set in stone. It can and hopefully will be changed.

We do a lot of book makeovers at Spirit Media®. Angela Simms' story is an amazing illustration of how a Spirit Media® makeover can make a huge difference in successful book marketing.

YOU CAN TOO
by Angela Cunningham Simms

When I met Angela, she was so embarrassed and disgraced. Not having a computer, she had written her book on her phone. Now that's incredible. She had big dreams and aspirations for her book. She told me how she had paid someone to publish her book, but when she saw it, she was so humiliated. It was full of grammatical errors. The cover was good but the layout was bad.

She immediately collected only one star reviews on Amazon. Needless to say, her book had not sold. Angela's story had been lost in the poor quality of her publishing. Instead of it being a celebration moment, Angela was full of shame and disgrace.

Angela said, "One of my grandchildren was accidentally left out of the book." Angela begged us to pray it could be republished.

Someone overhearing the conversation came forward and contributed a scholarship for Spirit Media® to republish Angela's book. And she burst into tears when I told her.

Our team went to work. As we listened to Angela, she kept saying, "I wrote this book and told my story of overcoming to help others see that, with Jesus: you can too!" This became the title of her book.

We re-edited her entire book, perfecting it to the Chicago Manual of Style. We wrote a killer book description and author bio using specific keywords that will help her book to sell.

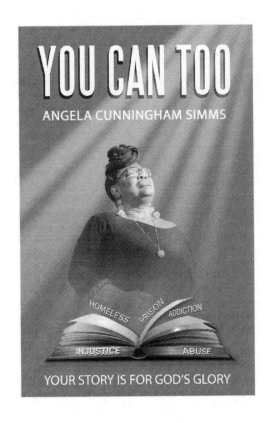

We used a fresh and feminine layout that readers would love.

When we finished, her book was beautiful, well organized, and sprinkled with marketing keywords to help her book sell. And now we can report that her updated book sales have jumped to many times more with this version . . . and climbing.

At Spirit Media® we only want to publish books the world will love to read. Publishing and getting it to market is NOT our goal. That's too small a vision. Our goal is to publish every book to be an international bestseller. We believe that the message of God through the people of God is worthy to be published to the nations.

Angela's book passed these quality standards. We are proud to publish Angela's book.

The good news is, Angela is now able to hold her head high and be proud of her book.

Here is one industry secret everyone needs to understand: authors, NOT publishers, sell books.

All traditional publishers who write a check for an author's manuscript are going to calculate the amount based on the author's marketing ability, NOT their quality of publishing. A book's value is on the author, not the publisher.

A traditional publisher is going to pay the author an advance based upon that author's marketing ability. Yes, the publisher will do the marketing and the publisher will receive at least 70% of the profits.

On average, the author gets paid only $.70 per book. The publisher keeps the rest. It's great business for the publisher, but it's lousy business for the author. The difference is the publisher does the marketing for the author in order to back up their investment. And marketing is the difference.

The value to the publisher is the author. A good publisher is able to double, triple, and multiply every dollar paid to the author. Why? Because authors, not publishers, sell books. Take the author out of the equation and the publisher has ZERO profits.

The difference between a $10,000 advance and a $1M dollar advance is the author's marketing potential.

Authors, not publishers, sell books.

The reason the vast majority of books sell fewer than 250 copies is because the vast majority of authors are waiting for a publisher to market their books. The fallacy is that publishers sell books, but this is not true unless the author has hired a publisher to sell their books. Most books are put on the market without any marketing strategy. This means 99% of books are not selling.

The best time for an author to take responsibility for marketing their book is while they're writing their book. This marketing strategy can never stop.

The next example illustrates the reality of this key, "When marketing stops, sales stop".

Escaping Anxiety by Dr James E. Kilgore

When Jim contacted us, he shared how he had used a well known Christian book publisher to publish his book in 2019, but it was not selling. So he asked us to take a look at it. He sent us a copy and we immediately saw a "typical Christian cover" but not a "WOW! cover."

We also saw that he had content gold all throughout his book. One obvious problem we found is that his cover did NOTHING to market this gold in his book.

Jim has four decades of experience as a minister, marriage counselor, and Sunday school teacher. He's authored numerous books, one of which, *Try Marriage Before Divorce*, had sold over 200,000 copies back in the 1980s. That's a huge accomplishment.

So why wasn't his new book selling? We found three primary reasons:

1. It was put on the market but never marketed.

2. It wasn't published with marketing in mind.

3. The cover gave a lousy representation of the gold within this book.

Here's what we did:

1. We listened to Jim. We captured his conviction that this was a message from God for the nations.

2. We also captured his keywords.

3. We identified his "why." Jim wrote this book so people could find freedom from their fear, doubts, and worries.

4. We retitled the book and led with Jim's why: *Escaping Anxiety*.

5. We wrote a killer book description and author bio integrating keywords that resonate with readers. In doing so, we emphasized Jim, the author, because authors sell books.

6. We added a table of contents so readers can see where they are going.

7. We gave it a fresh layout.

People are Googling the word "anxiety" far more than any other word. Books that sell are found.

You need to do whatever it takes for your book to be found.

When we finished it looked like a completely different book. It is 90% the same, but the 10% we revised moved it from good to GREAT. It will definitely sell now.

The new title, *Escaping Anxiety*, is much more culturally relevant than the former title, *Living Without Limits*. Most people do not wake up asking how do I live without limits today? Millions of people are asking how they can escape anxiety.

Here's the comparison of keyword searches we found:

Living - 301,100

Without - 18,100

Limits - 49,500

Escaping - 90,500

Anxiety - 450,000

More about keywords soon, but that's why we do a lot of book makeovers.

If you have already published your book and are not interested in a book makeover, then let this chapter give you a vision for your next book.

Let's now discuss another key aspect that helps your book be found.

Your Cover is a Key Marketing Opportunity.

You have less than five seconds to sell someone on your book through your book cover. Imagine that your book is in a bookstore sitting beside 1,000 other books. If your cover doesn't jump out at people in an ocean of other books then you've missed the opportunity to be purchased and read. That's marketing.

Your cover MUST pop. It must command attention. It must engage potential readers.

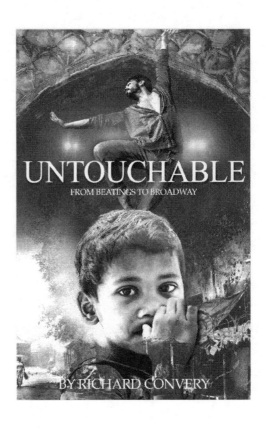

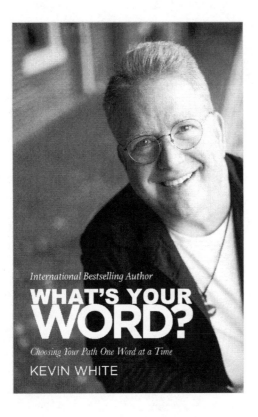

The back cover of your book MUST address why someone would want to read your book. If you don't answer, "What's in it for me?" then it is not going to sell.

American author and inspirational speaker Simon Sinek says, "People don't buy what you do. They buy why you do it." (Sinek, n.d.) This is true of books too. Why should I read your book? Don't focus on what your book is. Instead, focus on why your book matters to me.

Your Introduction is a Key Marketing Opportunity.

In your introduction you need to tell me what is at stake if I don't read this book. What will I miss if I don't? What will I gain if I do read it? Every reader in the world is asking, "What's in it for ME?" Like it or hate it, you must address this if you want your book to sell.

Your Chapter Titles Are a Key Marketing Opportunity.

When a reader flips through your book, and they will, your chapter titles better sell them on the value of reading your book. If they see value, they will read it. If they don't then they will not even start. If they read until chapter four but don't see value in chapter five, they will stop reading it. We all have. Every chapter either adds value or is missing the opportunity.

Books that sell must *sell*.

A book that sells never stops selling. It sells on the front cover, back cover, and everywhere in between. It sells in the introduction and all the way to the conclusion. It sells with each chapter title and throughout every chapter. It never stops selling.

While our authors are writing their books, we provide them with several tools to help them begin to think about book marketing.

One tool our authors love is our book outline template. It will absolutely help you outline your book, but even more importantly, it will help you draft a vision for your book.

Spirit Media's Book Outline Template Tool

Here are the questions from our tool:

1. How do you want your book to serve your readers? What will they get out of it?

2. Imagine it's two years after your book was published, and we're looking back on the results together. What's the book done for you that made the effort worthwhile?

3. What is the single event that will happen because of the book that will cause you to break out the champagne and celebrate?

4. Who Is your primary audience? (Who do you want to be here for?)

5. Under which category of books on Amazon will your book be listed?

6. Describe a typical person in your primary audience (your soul reader). Give them a name, describe them as you would describe any real person you know. Who are they, what do they do, where are they in their life, etc.?

7. What pain is this person experiencing because they've not read your book?

8. What transformation will this person get in their life because they read and implemented your book?

9. In one paragraph (150 words max), complete these thoughts:

10. This book is about . . . (the premise).

11. It's for . . . (the audience).

12. It will deliver . . . (the promise).

13. What's the "cocktail party pitch" of your book (i.e., the one-sentence explanation your ideal reader would actually use to recommend your book to their friends)?

14. Write this sentence with your positioning and make sure this is the book you want to write.

15. "I will use my book to target [primary audience], by teaching them [book idea], which will lead to my ultimate goal of more [objectives]."

16. Is that the book you want to write?

    If yes, you are ready to outline.

    If not, then get with an editor and work on it with them.

We guide our authors to answer these questions before they even start outlining their book.

Vision is marketing. Marketing is vision.

Once you have a vision for your book, then outlining it will be easy. But without vision, outlining it will be impossible. Once our authors answer these questions, then we provide them with worksheets to outline their chapter titles and each chapter itself.

Within a short period of time, they have their entire book outlined. They will never experience writer's block, or not knowing what to write. They will be able to follow their outline and write their entire book.

We also provide our authors with a Keyword Questionnaire Tool that helps pull the keywords out for them.

We can pull keywords out of websites and out of books. Why pull keywords when you can intentionally plant keywords? While we do not want to become obnoxious about keywords, we absolutely do need to know and respect the keywords our potential readers are searching.

Spirit Media's Keyword Questionnaire Tool

Here are the questions and descriptions we guide our authors to answer:

1. What makes your heart sing and energizes you the most?

2. What are the top three ways you're known for helping people?

3. List three reasons you are writing your book.

4. Please write three possible taglines.

5. What phrase(s) will your potential readers Google in order to find your book?

6. List up to twenty-five top words that best represent/describe the content of your book.

7. Narrow this list down to the top ten words.

8. Narrow this list down to the top five words.

9. Narrow this list down to the top 3 words.

10. When someone sees your book and walks away, what is the one phrase you want them to confidently declare?

11. If not already stated, what's the bottom line of your book? If your audience can only remember one thing, what would it be?

12. Do you have any final thoughts to share about your book?

If you wait until your book goes live on Amazon to start marketing it, you are already behind. Marketing begins as soon as you accept the assignment to start writing a book. Don't let this discourage or overwhelm you. It will actually make your book better.

Are you ready for the cold hard truth?

You're either a good marketer or a bad marketer, but you are a marketer. You can either fight it or embrace it. I hope you will embrace it. Say it, "I am a marketer." Add this, "I am a great marketer." By the end of this book that will be true.

Now, let's look at why it's so important to know who to market your book to.

If you're an author, you're a marketer.

2

CHAPTER

Publish to the Nations

The No. 1 reason most books don't sell is that they are published with too small of a vision.

At Spirit Media® we publish in EVERY format EVERYWHERE worldwide. Why? Because . . .

- We are called.

- We can.

We Are Called.

Psalm 96:3 (NLT) says, "Publish his glorious deeds among the nations. Tell everyone the great things he does."

The "nations" are not limited to simply the United States, or even North America.

John Wesley, a theologian and evangelist in the 1700s, said, "The world is my parish."

While you need to know your niche, you also need to respect that your niche is spread all over the world. If you're writing a cookbook, then write it for cooks. The good news is there are cooks in every family worldwide.

Because we are called, we publish books in every format simultaneously: paperback, hardback, eBook, and audiobooks.

And at Spirit Media®, publishing is way more than just book publishing. We publish:

- Brands
- Podcast Shows (video & audio)
- Websites
- Live Broadcasts
- Articles
- Blogs
- Social Media
- YouTube Channels
- Videos
- Radio Spots
- TV Spots
- and more . . .

Every time you post a social media post, you are publishing. Every time you upload a video to YouTube, you are asked if you want to publish it. When you write a blog, it begins in draft mode and eventually you publish it. Publishing is way more than putting a book on the market.

We Can.

We live in a day where it is possible to sell your book in all twenty-five Amazon Marketplaces around the world. No doubt more marketplaces will be added soon. There are over thirty eBook stores worldwide. There are over forty audiobook stores worldwide. Why limit the marketing of your book to 4% of readers living in the USA when it is possible to market your book to 100% of readers worldwide?

Because we can, Spirit Media® publishes in EVERY format everywhere. This means worldwide—everywhere on Amazon. All major eBook stores. All major audiobook stores. Your website(s). Your events. Truly, the distribution opportunities are endless.

AMAZON MARKETPLACES

1. Amazon Australia (amazon.com.au)
2. Amazon Belgium (amazon.com.be)
3. Amazon Brazil (amazon.com.br)
4. Amazon Canada (amazon.ca)
5. Amazon Egypt (amazon.eg)
6. Amazon France (amazon.fr)
7. Amazon Germany (amazon.de)
8. Amazon India (amazon.in)
9. Amazon Italy (amazon.it)
10. Amazon Japan (amazon.jp)
11. Amazon Mexico (amazon.com.mx)

12. Amazon Netherlands (amazon.nl)

13. Amazon Poland (amazon.pl)

14. Amazon Saudi Arabia (amazon.sa)

15. Amazon Singapore (amazon.sg)

16. Amazon Spain (amazon.es)

17. Amazon Sweden (amazon.se)

18. Amazon Turkey (amazon.com.tr)

19. Amazon United Arab Emirates (amazon.ae)

20. Amazon United Kingdom (amazon.co.uk)

21. Amazon United States (amazon.com)

22. South Africa – Feb, 2023

23. Colombia – Feb, 2023

24. Nigeria- Apr, 2023

25. Chile – Apr, 2023

GLOBAL eBOOK DISTRIBUTION NETWORKS

1. Amazon Kindle

2. Kobo

3. American Booksellers Association (variety of participant websites)

4. Angus & Robertson (Australia)

5. Bol (Netherlands)

6. Bookworld (Australia – formerly Borders AU)

7. Collins (Australia)

8. Eason (Ireland)

9. FNAC (France)

10. FNAC (Portugal)

11. Indigo (Canada)

12. La Central (Spain)

13. La Feltrinelli (Italy)

14. Livraria Cultura (Brazil)

15. Mondadori (Italy)

16. National Book Store (Philippines)

17. Orbile (Mexico)

18. PaperPlus (New Zealand)

19. PriceMinister (France)

20. Rakuten (Japan)

21. WHSmith (UK)

22. Apple iBookstore

23. Google eBooks

24. Barnes & Noble

25. Scribd

26. Tolino

27. OverDrive

28. Bibliotheca

29. Baker & Taylor

30. BorrowBox

31. Hoopla

32. Vivlio

GLOBAL AUDIOBOOK DISTRIBUTORS

1. Amazon
2. Audible
3. Apple iTunes
4. Barnes & Noble Nook
5. Google Play
6. Kobo/Walmart
7. 24symbols
8. Anyplay
9. Audiobooks.com
10. AudiobooksNow
11. AudiobooksNZ
12. Authors Direct
13. BajaLibros
14. Beek
15. Bokus
16. BookBeat
17. Bookmate
18. Chirp
19. Downpour
20. eStories
21. Fuuze

22. Hibooks
23. Hummingbird
24. Digital Media
25. Instaread
26. Leamos
27. Libro.fm
28. Nextory
29. Papaya FM
30. Layster
31. Scribd
32. Storytel
33. 3Leaf Group
34. Axiell Media
35. Baker & Taylor
36. Bibliotheca
37. Bidi
38. EBSCO
39. Follett
40. Hoopla MLOL
41. Odilo
42. OverDrive
43. Perma-Bound Wheelers

When I published my first book, *Audacious Generosity*, I was equally as concerned about reaching India with it as I was about reaching the United States.

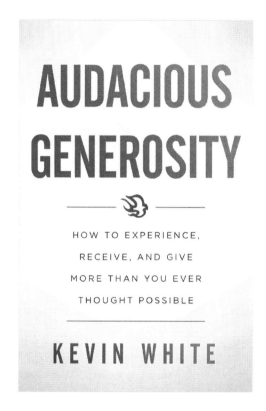

For the previous twelve years I flew over a million miles and traveled to India over fifty times. I've seen firsthand that a printed book is a luxury in most homes in India.

India is the most read country in the world. (World Population Review, 2023) They outread all other countries including the United States. But, most publishers (including Christian publishers) only concentrate on the U.S. market. This reaches a whopping 4% of world readers. Today, we can do better than that.

It took me a while, but I figured out how to produce and publish *Audacious Generosity* as an audiobook. I knew that if there was any hope of getting *Audacious Generosity* into the hands of internationals, it would need to include both eBook and audiobook formats. Most publishers treat audiobooks as an add-on. At Spirit Media® we include audiobooks in our basic publishing package. Our goal is to publish every book in paperback, hardback, eBook, and audiobook everywhere books are sold worldwide.

The difference between you selling 250 copies and 250,000 copies is vision.

The truth is, you can sell what you decide to sell. God has made it possible for you to sell your book in Australia. Are you? Will you? It may not be easy, but it is possible.

What's your vision? Right now, define your specific goal (number of sales) for selling your book.

Your goals should be SMART:

S = Specific – concrete action, step-by-step actions needed to reach the goal

M = Measurable – observable results from the accomplishment of the goal

A = Attainable – the goal is both possible and is done at the right time with sufficient attention and resources

R = Realistic – the probability of success is good, given the resources and attention put forth

T = Time-bound – the goal is achieved within a specified period of time (three years) in a way that takes advantage of the opportunity before it passes you by.

The message of God through you is worthy to be published to the nations. Make sure your vision is God-size. God wouldn't say publish to the nations if it were not possible. Where God guides He provides.

God's vision for your book is to the nations. Next we will look at God's strategy.

> **"People are not lazy. They simply have impotent goals. That is – goals that do not inspire them."**
> **- Tony Robbins**

CHAPTER

Generosity Marketing

When a new restaurant opens up, the management will host a private opening before the grand opening. They will invite guests to come in and eat for free in order to train their staff and make sure all their systems are in place before they open up to the public.

This is one form of generosity marketing. The guests for this private opening help create a buzz for the grand opening.

Every time you go to Costco, Sam's Club, and BJ's Wholesale you will find product samples. This is another form of generosity marketing. These samples whet your appetite for more. A free sample can turn into a purchase. Not only that, but stand and watch and you'll see customers influencing other customers to sample the product. Generosity marketing can quickly go viral.

When I was marketing my books, I committed to giving away thousands of copies in order to sell millions of copies. It cost very little to give away the eBook version.

As Executive Director of Global Hope India, I knew it would be advantageous to use my books as a thank-you gift to our donors.

In June 2021, I figured out how to get a bulk printing of my first book, *Audacious Generosity*. Like many authors, I had been purchasing as many copies through print on demand as I could afford. Print on demand was costing over $8 per paperback. By bulk printing 2,000 paperback copies, I got the price down to less than $3 per copy.

I donated copies to Global Hope India and we sent out over 500 thank-you gifts to potential donors.

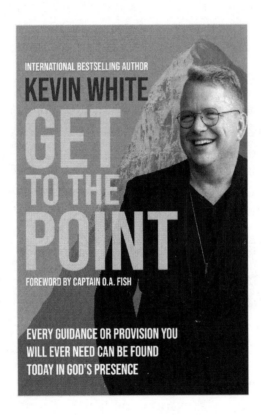

On November 9, 2021, Spirit Media® published my second book, *Get to the Point*, in paperback, hardback, eBook, and audiobook—simultaneously, everywhere, worldwide—and we put over 700 copies in the mail that day. It was better, faster, and for less cost than I had paid for *Audacious Generosity*. That's when Spirit Media® was born. I knew God had given us something great.

I was so busy juggling leading Global Hope India and sending out my books that I had not even considered the impact of sending out thank-you gifts to potential donors.

In mid-January 2022, God led me to calculate donations from people who had received one or both of our gifts in 2021. I calculated actual donations Global Hope India had received. Over $150,000 was donated from people who had received one or both of my books. It gets better. Of the $150,000, over $111,000 was received from donors who had never given to Global Hope India before. Needless to say, I was blown away.

After two decades focused on missions in India, my books drip with passion for God's work in India. They are great resource tools for Global Hope India.

In *Audacious Generosity*, I shared God's strategy of generosity and the impact of generosity. One of the best marketing strategies in the world is generosity. It's been God's strategy since the very beginning. John 3:16 says, "God so loved that he gave..." God is the king of generosity marketing.

If you haven't already, I highly recommend you read my book, *Audacious Generosity*. Every wise marketer in the world needs a solid understanding of God's strategy of generosity. It will absolutely revolutionize your marketing.

"Practical tips, empowering questions, & spiritual wisdom"
— Judy Greenman, Founder, BodyBrainFreedom.com

the cost of printing 2,000 copies. That's the power of generosity marketing.

Generosity marketing works.

In the chapters that follow, you'll see your need for book reviews, podcast show interviews, and more. I strongly recommend you approach all these opportunities with generosity marketing in mind.

One of the easiest ways to collect book reviews is to give away copies of your book in exchange for reviews.

Don't consider it a failure to give your book away. Actually, it's genius. And, don't be prideful thinking anyone reading your book must pay.

Barbara Hemphill is one of the most successful entrepreneurs I've ever met. She used to kick herself because she built her businesses by giving away her books. When we published her latest book, *Walking with Barbara: 30 Emails from God*, I encouraged her to sell it worldwide but offer it to everyone she could for free.

Barbara has a compassion project in India called Shepherd House Ministry. She printed 2,000 paperback copies of her book with a goal to raise $75,000 for The Shepherd's House. Today, she is giving away copies of her book and inviting everyone to donate toward her compassion project. The average paperback book sells for $15. Barbara is regularly receiving donations. Barbara has already received in donations more than

Nothing is for free.

When it comes to generosity marketing, value is very important. You're reducing the cost, not the value of your book. Every book I give away clearly communicates its value. While it's a gift, it's not free. Every book costs me to write, publish, print, package, and mail. Nothing is free.

John 3:16 (NIV) says, "For God so loved the world that he gave his one and only Son. . . -" This represents a free gift to the world, but it is a very costly gift. Actually, it's the most valuable gift you can ever receive.

Always communicate the value of what you're giving away.

A true gift is given without any strings attached.

At the same time, always give without strings attached.

John 3:16 also represents that God took a risk by offering His gift. Reject it or receive it, His offer stands. God's free gift is without any strings attached. It will set you free to recognize this. Don't give to manipulate or control. Give to bless. Give to give, not to receive. Motive is very important, and we can all smell impure motives a mile away.

Communicate the value. Give in exchange for reviews. But at the end of the day, always give without any strings attached.

You will never outgive God.

Generosity marketing does NOT mean you only give away your book. Don't be afraid to sell your book. Expect your book to sell. Make it easy for people to buy it. Market to sell.

If you're uncomfortable selling your book, then find a coach, mentor, therapist, or whatever you need and work through it.

Sometimes we think God needs our help so we give away all our books. This is as unbalanced as refusing to be generous. Let there be balance. Don't be ashamed to make a profit. Actually, it's dishonoring to God to be in business and be afraid to make a profit. Like it or not, the call to write is a call to business, marketing, and getting God's message to the nations.

I encourage you to expect God to empower you to succeed at writing, business, marketing, and getting God's message to the nations. He is able. Let him do it through you for His glory.

The truth is, He's got your back. Keep this in mind as we discuss in the next chapter another dynamic aspect of successful book marketing: backing your book with your brand.

CHAPTER

Back it with a Brand

Books are written by authors. Every author is a brand.

The difference between a Big Mac and a Whopper is the brand. Both are cheeseburgers. Both have sold millions. Both are served as fast food. When you want a Big Mac, you look for the Golden Arches. Big Macs are distributed by McDonald's.

Imagine if every McDonald's restaurant was branded differently—what if some were Big Mac, others were Chicken Nuggets, and others were Vanilla Shakes. The brand is McDonald's. Each McDonald's offers the same common menu items. The menu has changed some over the years, but the brand is very consistent. Look for the Golden Arches and you'll find a Big Mac.

The same is true of Whoppers. When you want a Whopper you look for Burger King. The Brand is Burger King.

As an author, YOU are a brand. You're either a good brand or a bad brand for your book, but YOU are the brand.

In the same way you can't imagine the Big Mac without McDonald's, you need to connect your book(s) with your brand.

Every time McDonald's is marketed, so is the Big Mac. You can market a cheeseburger without marketing McDonald's, but you can't market McDonald's without marketing the Big Mac. The same is true of you.

Market your brand and you'll market your book(s). Your book(s) may come and go, but your brand is what stays consistent, just like McDonald's Golden Arches.

Branding and marketing are similar, yet different.

Marketing can be a short-term campaign, but branding takes a long-term commitment.

No book should be without a brand.

No brand should be without a book.

One of the best things I ever did to advance Global Hope India as a global thought leader in India missions was to begin writing books.

Five years earlier, we had a strategic planning meeting at Global Hope India and developed a strategy to position Global Hope India as a global thought leader in India missions. During that planning session we discussed the vision of GHI providing content that would make us known as a global thought leader.

I went away knowing the need for content. It wasn't until I wrote my first book that I got it.

Authors not organizations, write books.

Global Hope India has done a masterful job of providing content, but nothing positioned GHI as a global thought leader until I started writing books. Like I've said, my books drip with passion for God's work in India. When I published my books, something happened that had not yet happened by publishing:

- Websites

- Blogs

- Podcasts

- Social Media

- Business Collateral

- and more.

By publishing my books, I positioned myself as a leader in missions in India. This positioned Global Hope India as a trusted voice in missions in India.

When I say that authors write books, not organizations, I mean it. The most strategic way to position Global Hope India as a revered brand in India missions was for me to step forward as a global thought leader.

I learned a lot about branding by publishing my first book.

When *Audacious Generosity* went on the market, I was unknown. You couldn't find me on the internet. All of a sudden, I realized that it was going to be me, the author, and not the organization, that was going to sell books. That's when it hit me: authors, not organizations, write books.

That's when I committed to brand myself as the author. Within two months, I had a website and social media. I developed my own email list. That year I started hosting two livestream broadcasts per month. I launched a YouTube channel. I produced a monthly keynote message which we divided up into sixty second clips for my one-minute motivation series entitled "Generously Blessed."

I did it. I took the plunge to be a content creator. I prayed and asked the Holy Spirit what He wanted to say to the nations. I committed to share whatever God gave me to share. I've never lacked content.

When God led me to write, He used Psalm 96:3 (NLT),

"Publish his glorious deeds among the nations. Tell everyone the great things he does."

I began to see that God was calling me not just to write but to publish. And, I began to understand this involved branding and marketing.

In less than two years I went from being unknown to being heard in over 166 different countries. My second book, *Get to the Point*, has sold over 2 million copies. Every month I receive royalties in my bank account from my books. My YouTube channel has grown now to be monetized. Every week people subscribe to my content through YouTube, social media, email, and SMS.

Now, that's branding. Actually, that is the power of branding.

Let me say it again: one of the best things I've ever done to further the ministry of Global Hope India was to begin writing books. Every book needs a brand and every brand needs a book.

You have the opportunity to do the same for your organization, business, or church. One of the best things you will ever do to build your business, church, or organization is to publish a book.

Spirit Media® began on the success of my books. We don't just hope to make our clients successful, we know we will make our clients successful. We are reinventing publishing in three very specific and strategic ways:

1. Connecting publishing and branding together.

2. Marketing before publishing.

3. Publishing in every format everywhere.

The foundation of this revolution is branding. We back our books with branding. Either one without the other is weak. No book should be without a brand. No brand should be without a book.

If you are serious about your brand, then you need to contact us today about starting your book. We will meet you and your content wherever you are. Please let me explain.

We Hand You Your Manuscript

Gone are the days of authors slipping away for a 2-3 month sabbatical to write their book. Another truth is that many content creators are too busy creating content to write a book. That's why Spirit Media® takes your content and turns it into books for you.

At Spirit Media®, you don't have to hand your manuscript to us in order to publish a book. Give us the opportunity and we will hand your manuscript to you. We can take your previously recorded video and audio files, transcribe them, and edit them into chapters of a book.

Take, for instance, a pastor's sermon series or a corporate trainer's training program. If you have ten podcast episodes, you have ten chapters of a book. And the average book has ten chapters.

It's literally your message in your own words. Let us write your manuscript for you. This is just another way we are transforming the publishing industry.

Commit to Content Creation

When it comes to branding, you need to commit. As an author, you have created content. You have a book. Now you need to commit to being a content creator. God's message through you is much bigger than just one book. Here are some of the ways you can build your brand:

1. Publish a book.

2. Publish a blog.

3. Launch a podcast show.

4. Start a YouTube channel.

5. Create an email subscription.

6. Grow your social media presence.

7. Host a livestream broadcast.

8. Host virtual training events.

9. Host in-person events.

10. Be a speaker.

Your brand is the mouth for your message. Lipstick can be sexy, but it's the message that moves the brand forward.

Commit to:

1. Being a content creator

2. Publishing your message to the nations

3. Using every format you can

And your brand will grow. Back your book(s) with your brand and it will help your book(s) to sell.

Make sure your brand is:

1. Clear

2. Compelling

3. Consistent

This is a book, in and of itself. Let me be brief.

By clear, I mean you are the brand. Not your one book or video. Be clear who/what your brand is. Going back to the example of McDonald's, imagine if one location was named chicken nuggets, the next location was named French fries, and on and on. That would be ridiculous, yet many authors do this to themselves. Be clear. Know your brand and your audience will know your brand.

Be compelling. Make sure you offer one easy to follow call-to-action at a time:

1. Subscribe to my YouTube channel

2. Buy my book

3. Attend my event

An effective brand engages followers. Be compelling.

By being consistent, I mean know your Golden Arches and use them consistently. Golden Arches are yellow, not hot pink. Your face, logo, color, and styling needs to be consistent everywhere. Your sound bites need to be consistent. Your calls-to-action need to be consistent.

Make sure your brand is clear, compelling, and consistent—and it will grow.

In the next chapters we will reveal amazing practical steps necessary to sell your book. But let's put the foundational principles together and quickly review the first four key concepts. It's so helpful to keep these in mind while learning how to make it happen.

Start Marketing While Writing.

For successful book marketing, it's crucial to start with this mindset: start marketing while writing. From the beginning, including every chapter title and subtitle, to every explanation, your reader needs to stay motivated with the value of your content.

Publish to the Nations.

That means that we carefully identify our reader but we recognize that our market and mission vision includes the whole world. Our God-appointed goal is to fulfill the words of Psalm 96:3 (NLT), "Publish His glorious deeds among the nations. Tell everyone the great things He does." God's message entrusted to you is definitely needed in the whole world.

Embrace Generosity Marketing

God models His awesome giving heart to us, but He also extends blessings to those who will follow Him by pursuing generous giving. Generosity marketing opens more doors, earns more sales, and reaches more people with God's message than we imagine possible. He " . . . supplies seed to the sower and bread to the eater" (2 Corinthians 9:10). Yes, His generous blessing extends to both our readers and to us through generosity marketing.

Market Your Brand.

The fourth foundational principle is . . . you. Yes, you, your passion, your organization, are your brand. Market your brand and you'll market your book.

Keep these four foundational principles in mind (consider them often) as we embark in the next chapters on discovering the specific steps necessary to successfully market your brand and your book.

CHAPTER

Grow Your Contact List

Professional marketers (the experts with the master's degree in marketing) repeatedly say that a good email list is a business' best asset for bottom-line sales. Book sales is a business.

Statistical surveys consistently reveal that at least 59% of consumers say marketing emails influence their purchasing decisions (hubspot.com). Several other marketing studies attribute $42 in sales revenue earned for every $1 spent on email strategies. Marketing professionals resolutely stress that email marketing in today's market is imperative.

Please let us say it another way. To sell your book you need subscribers.

A high-quality email list is the No. 1 way to grow and reach new subscribers who will buy your book.

Many experienced authors highly recommend that new independent authors start building an email list and marketing one year prior to the publication date. "Do it now." is their mantra.

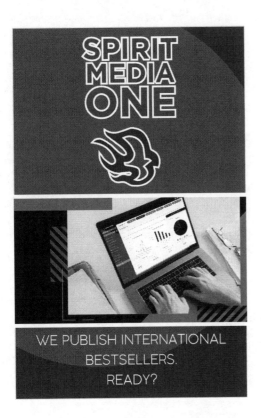

WE PUBLISH INTERNATIONAL BESTSELLERS. READY?

Here's the good news. The Spirit Media® ONE platform streamlines and accelerates building and managing your email list. It makes it so much easier and effective, without the cost and time required for that master's degree.

In this chapter we discuss fundamental essentials to help you grow an essential and powerful email list in your niche. Remember: The Spirit Media® ONE platform greatly assists with accomplishing every one of these tasks.

1. **Regularly share your message.**

   Create and send regular short emails to your subscribers to share your unique message. This might include a short story from your book, a helpful key idea (verse), or a testimonial from someone whose life was positively impacted by reading your book. Be inspirational.

   At first this may seem difficult, but there's a great reason why it's easy for you. You've got a calling and a great message. The fire and passion of that calling will empower you. You sincerely want to help your constituency. Just talk to them like talking to a friend. Simply connect with their heart about your special message, focus, and passion.

   It's best not to be academic but to be conversational and passionate. Your subscribers really need what you have on an everyday level. This opens the door to selling more books, which will minister to more people. That's what it's all about.

   (Go ahead. Say it. "I have a message. I can do this.")

2. **Encourage email sharing.**

   Your subscribers will often know someone else who will appreciate or need your story that day.

   It's easy to encourage email sharing by including an "Email to a Friend." button at the bottom of your email. Don't forget to also include a "Subscribe" button at the bottom so their friend can opt-in as well. This will amazingly widen and increase your message and book's impact. The Spirit Media® ONE team will help you accomplish this easy task.

3. **Create multiple targeted subscriber types.**

This is easily accomplished by segmenting your email list into groups according to buyer persona. When creating focused, special messages to segmented buyers within your broader niche, it increases the chance of their interest peaking to the point of subscribing and buying your book. This list builds and builds over time.

4. **Do you have employees?**

Add an opt-in link to your employees' signatures. These hyperlinked email signatures can lead people to a landing page where they can sign up for your mailing list and find your book.

5. **Create a new lead-generation offer or tool that requires sign-up.**

Lead generation is the process of attracting subscribers by nurturing their interest and trust. This may be accomplished by offering them valuable and helpful content like a free blog membership, discount coupons for your book, a free webinar/class or event, or even a free short eBook. Whatever it is, they will provide their email and contact information, and you just earned a new subscriber lead.

Amazing growth of your email list will happen when using social media.

6. Hosting an online contest is a great way to promote your book and engage with your subscribers. To get started, you'll need to decide what you'll be giving away. It could be a free product, a discount, or even just a fun prize.

Once you've decided on the prize, it's time to create the rules of the contest. Be sure to include how to enter, as well as explaining eligibility requirements. For example, you may want to require participants to provide a fun or interesting comment about your book topic.

Once you have the details worked out, it's time to start promoting the contest. Use social media, email, and even word-of-mouth to spread the word and get people excited about entering.

And that's it. With a little effort, you can host a successful online contest that will help promote your book, build customer relationships, and build your email subscribers list.

7. 🐦 Twitter is a unique way to generate leads with a particular type of person within your niche. There are a few key things to accomplish to make sure your campaign is successful.

First, consider running a giveaway. Everyone loves free stuff, so this is a great way to get people's attention. Make sure the prize is relevant to your offer and be sure to include your contact information so that people can easily find you.

Using creative images and snappy hashtags will also make your campaign stand out. Just a few simple steps will definitely generate valuable leads using Twitter.

8. 📘 Leveraging the power of Facebook is one of the best ways to grow your email list. This method can exponentially multiply the number of email subscribers. Here are four powerful tips:

A. For your Facebook profile cover photo, make your email newsletter the image displayed. Make sure it's visually appealing.

B. The cover photo also needs a call-to-action (CTA) button that encourages people to sign up for your newsletter.

C. Include landing page links. In each newsletter, include links to your website's opt-in landing pages. This will make it easy for people to sign up for your newsletter.

D. Use newsletter snippets. In each newsletter, include short snippets of content from your blog or website. This will give people a taste of what they can expect from your newsletter and encourage them to sign up.

9. ▶️ In today's marketing environment, creating YouTube videos is one of the most powerful ways to generate leads. Don't overlook this one. By utilizing engagement features like end screens and video outros, it encourages viewers to take action to subscribe to your YouTube channel, visit your website, or take advantage of a special offer for your book. Plus, YouTube makes it easy to add a CTA button to videos, making it even simpler for viewers to take the next step. When used effectively, YouTube videos can be a powerful lead generation tool that can increase your book sales.

10. 📷 Instagram is also a significant social media tool for generating quality leads. By including a CTA button on your posts and a link to a sign-up form in your bio, it makes it easy for people to get more information about your book.

Use Instagram Stories to drive traffic to your website or landing page. Simply create a story with a CTA such as "swipe up to learn more" and add a link to your website or sign-up form. When done correctly, Instagram can be an amazingly effective way to grow your email list.

11. Guest blogging is a great way to generate leads for your book sales. By writing short articles from your book's content for other blogs, you can get exposure to new audiences and build awareness about your book. When done correctly, guest blogging will be a powerful lead generation tool for you.

    The first step is to identify the blogs that your target audience is reading. Once you've identified a few potential guest blogging opportunities, reach out to the blog owners and present your book and focused article idea. If they're interested, send them a draft of your article and include a CTA button at the end that links to your website or landing page.

    Guest blogging is a great way to get exposure to new audiences and build relationships with other bloggers in your niche specialty. By taking the time to present quality article ideas and including a CTA button, you can turn guest blogging into a powerful lead generation tool for your book sales.

Building an email list is both an essential and incredibly powerful tool for you, the author. Many professional marketers consider it the No. 1 way to reach your audience. Your email list is really the only thing entirely under your control and can win for you a community of lifelong fans and supporters, and an ongoing income from book sales. Go for it.

Now, let's proceed to another strategy that will literally multiply your strength and number of actions completed. How? By recruiting and building a promo team.

6

CHAPTER

Recruit a Promo Team

When an author releases a new book, it's essential to do more than just publish and hope for the best. There's no sense in performing like an unprepared surfer who bravely jumps on the next BIG wave. That's guaranteed wipeout.

The fact is, authors who sell more than 250 books have carefully implemented smart strategies to market and promote their book. The first essential step is to create a support team that can help you with every aspect of your strategic marketing efforts. This team is called a Launch Team. These wonderful people on your team will be so supportive, will help drive forward your marketing efforts with greater ease, and will become indispensable to your success.

What is a book launch team?

A book launch team is a group of people who voluntarily agree to help an author promote their book, particularly during the countdown time, up to its release. A good launch team provides powerful impetus toward spreading the word about your book. They are a great help to reach a larger audience. To build an effective launch team for your book, here are a few things to keep in mind.

Who is included on an effective book launch team?

An effective launch team helps promote a book during its launch period. This team can include the author's friends and family, beta readers, church friends, online social media group(s) members, and anyone else who is willing to help spread the word about your book. Sometimes you will find a person with launch team experience. If they can be supportive and work with you well, they can be a jewel for the successful release of your book.

What size should a good launch team be?

The size of a launch team varies depending on the book and the author's goals for the launch. A large launch team with a greater variety of special assignments can be immeasurably helpful in generating a positive buzz around the book. Of course, it's also important to make sure that everyone is genuinely interested in promoting the book.

Don't be overwhelmed. Even if your team is only you and two other people, you just tripled your reach.

It doesn't take hundreds of people to have an impact. Start small.

How to recruit your launch team?

It is important that the people you recruit know what you are asking them to do. Be specific about the task, goal, impact, and timeline. Are you asking them to commit to thirty days or one whole year? Will they be helping two hours a week or sixty hours a week?

Here's an example:

> Hey _____, my book releases in forty-five days. This book will help parents instill good habits into their children. Can you give a little time over the next month to secure commitments from thirty people who will leave a 5-star review on Amazon within the first week after launch? This will help advance my book on Amazon to thousands of people who don't yet know me.

Don't overcomplicate it, but do be clear and concise about what you're asking people to do for you.

How do I keep my launch team motivated?

OK. Here are some amazing tips compiled from previous authors to help keep your launch team genuinely interested in promoting your book.

9 Ways to Keep Your Launch Team Motivated.

1. Select team members who are

readers and buyers of books. This kind of person is naturally interested and easier to keep motivated.

2. Select team members with a connected, vested interest in your topic. If you are writing about something that will greatly help one of their immediate family members, that person will be more passionate about promoting your message. Thoughtfully consider how each team member may have a vested personal interest in your book's message, and how it helps them. When it comes time for video clips, they will provide a particularly effective and convincing testimony.

3. Be thankful in special ways. Continually let each one know how much you appreciate their participation. Isn't there a song that starts with, "Just a spoonful of sugar helps the . . . hmm, hmm, hmm"? Something like that.

4. Remember their birthday. A card, email, or even a small birthday party will bless them. (Blow noisy buzzers. Eat cake.)

5. At the beginning of the countdown, give them an Advanced Readers Copy (ARC) and sign it with a short comment of appreciation. This will become a treasure to discuss with their family for years. They will never tire of telling their family how they helped an author launch their book.

6. Make it easy for them to share your book on social media. Creating prewritten posts will help some, and others may particularly appreciate memes. Be creative.

7. Consider starting a launch team Facebook group for added communication and team interaction. Post their pictures.

8. Share special steps of accomplishments and progress related to your book. Sometimes they will have helpful suggestions about the cover, promotions, and other aspects of the development up to the release date.

9. Pray for them. Keep their hearts blessed and well fed.

And there you have it. Nine ways to keep your launch team motivated.

What assignments are essential for my launch team to accomplish?

The core BIG idea of launch team activity is promoting the message of your book. Before considering a list of promotion assignments, here are a few helpful pointers.

1. Make sure everyone is aware of their role and what is expected. Make it a challenge to accomplish. They will know better what to do, and their performance will be much more supportive and effective.

2. Discuss with team members how their assignment contributes to the whole. Often, it is helpful to do something like this in a general meeting.

3. Clearly identify deadlines for completion and how to report it to you.

4. Ask team members to let you know when they are involved with exciting, unscheduled conversations and opportunities to support your book's message. These might make very special testimonials and effective video clips so helpful to your people.

5. Create ongoing emails and posts as suggested materials they can use when talking about your book online or in person. This supports team members' clarity of thought and helps maintain integrity of message. Sometimes this is referred to as a "Swipe File."

What are some promotional assignments for your launch team members to accomplish?

- Make a master task list of the strategic marketing recommendations from this book. Find someone enthused to help you with different items on the list. Additionally, seriously consider the following comments . . .

- Ask them to share snippets or post photos from your book across social media and even with emails. Have them send you a screenshot or blind copy (bcc) you in emails. This keeps you in the loop and can help your motivation, as well. It also helps you monitor the content of comments for accuracy and agreement with your message.

- Ask members to submit positive reviews on Amazon. This creates a positive buzz and also may mitigate a few nasty comments from someone in the world who doesn't like your book.

- Find a team member who can manage your Amazon Kindle aspects. This will include items like crafting a great book listing, composing your author bio, choosing the best categories for your book, and monitoring and adjusting the best keywords for the message of your book. If you're a client of Spirit Media® we do this for you.

- Add their reviews to the "Goodreads Want to Read List." It is even more helpful to provide team members a how-to video, template, or tutorial to understand this process.

- Encourage them to share a book review on their YouTube channel. Some of the team members with a family or personal vested interest in your message will be especially impactful in a YouTube interview clip.

- Record a testimonial for your book. Do you have a team member that is a graphic designer or experienced and good at compiling a video? A clip of testimonials about your book could be powerful.

- Suggest they buy extra copies to give to their friends.

- Brainstorm. Ask your team members to give you more marketing ideas, such as a book trailer to help build up a buzz of excitement.

- Ask them to share the author's (your.) blog posts with friends, family, and others they think will love it.

- Ask them to recommend your book to their local library and let you know the response.

- Ask for assistance to schedule an online book launch party. If you're a client of Spirit Media® we do this for you.

- Perhaps one of your team members is a talented project manager and can coordinate a schedule of assignment activities to focus the team.

- Do you have a member that can compile and compose a team activities newsletter showcasing individuals, book awards, and activities?

- Find a team member that understands and is willing to help with press releases, ad campaigns, podcasting, and other professional methods of book promotion. If you have the budget, a PR agent can be worth the investment many times over.

Assembling a book launch team that will enthusiastically support your carefully planned schedule of promotions is a surefire way to multiply marketing efforts for your book. With a good launch team you are well on the way to riding that BIG wave, avoiding "wipeout," and selling a lot more than 250 books. A great deal more.

The next key action for exponentially greater book sales opens the window for potential customers to find your book. It's time to build a web page.

CHAPTER

Build a Web Page

There are many vital reasons why it is so beneficial for authors to obtain their own professional-looking and mobile-friendly website.

It's a dynamic way to reach out and personally connect to niche readers and followers with special news, blogs, and other valuable content. This helps them understand you and your work. You can better control the narrative about your book with a good website. You may have already heard this saying, but it's an axiom. . .

Communication with good content is king.

Your website is "the" platform to showcase your book. It allows you to sell it directly to readers, and to control the pricing and distribution of the publication.

Certainly, a website is a valuable marketing tool, reaching a wider audience to promote your work. Keeping all this in mind, it is highly recommended that the following items be included on your website, which itself is a benefit of our Spirit Media® ONE platform.

Publish your book's landing page on your website.

A landing page on your website is a dedicated page designed to encourage visitors to take a specific action. That will probably include buying your book or signing up for a mailing list.

When creating the landing page, be sure to include:

1. The book's title and cover image

2. A brief description of the book

3. A call-to-action (CTA) encouraging visitors to buy the book or sign up for your mailing list

By publishing your book's landing page on your website, you will reach a wider audience and generate increased interest.

Create a valuable blog on your website about your upcoming book.

In today's market, creating a blog is considered a particularly effective and engaging method to get the word out about your book. A blog provides a platform to share your book with the world and build excitement before and after its release.

A blog is a fun way to share excerpts, post behind-the-scenes photos, and conduct interviews with the key people of your work and life. It provides a digital window of connection with your readers and builds a community around your book.

However, it's important to make sure that blog content is more than just fun. It must add helpful value for readers, as well.

Fun content + value = memorable impact.

Regular and timely updates with fresh content keeps them coming back for more. Of course, that doesn't mean daily updates. Once-a-week is typically considered a normal, acceptable time period without becoming annoying. With a little effort, your blog will become a valuable asset to more readers and sell more books.

Create a countdown timer for the book's release date on your website.

As the release date for the much-anticipated book approaches, it is powerful to schedule a series of events. Create a countdown timer for the book's release date. This will build buzz, grow interest, and generate excitement in anticipation of the release.

A countdown schedule can easily be posted on social media, your website, and sent in a special email contact. The goal is to create a sense of urgency and to encourage people to pre-order the book or make plans to buy it on the day it comes out.

Set up an affiliate link to your Amazon page so you get commissions on book sales. Include sample chapters from your book on your website.

Setting up an affiliate link to your Amazon page should be on your to-do list of important ways to make extra money from book sales. And this tactic will help you earn commissions on any sales that are made through your link.

To get started, simply go to Amazon's website, and click on the "Join Associates" link at the bottom of the page. Then add your affiliate link to your book's sample chapters and any other articles you write. When people click on that link and purchase your book, you'll earn a commission on the sale. Affiliate commissions typically range from 4%-8%, so it's a great way to monetize your writing and boost your income from book sales.

After setting up your Amazon affiliate account, be sure to include sample chapters or excerpts from your book on your website.

Link to video clips about your book on your website.

If you're looking for a way to add some visuals to your website, video clips are a great option. In advance of the release date (and after), video clips will provide an overview of the book, and perhaps a short introduction of the author (you.). Plus, it's a great way for a potential reader to get a taste of the book before committing to buying and reading it. Be sure it includes a little bit of fun and is informative. Your readers won't be disappointed if you have good content, even if you don't feel like a movie star.

On your website, communicate directly with your email subscribers about new releases or your current blog post.

If you have subscribers to your blog or website, continually collecting email addresses is important.

That subscriber email list is a goldmine. Use it to directly communicate with your audience about new releases or your most recent blog post.

Although social media is a great platform for promoting your work, it's even more personal and impactful for email subscribers to see your message in their inbox that leads them to your website.

Email helps you craft a more personal message that speaks to the interests of your reader.

Of course, we don't want to spam our subscribers, so we keep messages relevant and interesting. Consistent message value makes readers always happy to hear from you, and positively impacts book sales. Social media is an important avenue to accomplish impactful messaging in today's book market.

And there you have it. Building a website page is an essential element of a successful book marketing strategy. It should include your book's landing page, a blog with helpful reading excerpts from your book, a countdown timer for your book's release date, and affiliate links to your Amazon book page. Don't forget to include a YouTube video and have pages to keep your readers up-to-date about recent developments before and after your book's release. All these elements will make your website dynamite and boost your book sales more and more.

At what point do the marketing professionals recommend that new authors build a good webpage? The maximum benefit providing the best public relations (PR) impact over time is one year before the book's release date.

Whew. That's a big job, but Spirit Media® can help you make an awesome and attractive website for your customers.

Once you have that awesome and attractive website that catches the attention of your buyers, it's time to take another step with your supportive team by getting people to talk about your message and book on social media.

CHAPTER

Get People Talking on Social Media

An integral part of a book marketing campaign in today's market is utilizing social media. Making social media effective is something like a good relationship. It requires an initial period of "getting to know you and me," as well as consistent communication.

A book marketing campaign that includes social media requires an author to be engaged, strategic, and enthused. To an author with a burning passion and message to help a particular audience, the benefits are awesome.

Here is a list of many important recommendations to make your social media marketing robust, effective, and profitable.

Select two social media sites

We've all heard it truly said, "The journey of a thousand miles begins with one step." One step. That truism uniquely applies to marketing a book when utilizing social media. It's so easy to feel responsible to be everywhere at once spreading our efforts, time, and energy too thin. Attempting to get too far too fast can be exhausting and discouraging. So, we have a few recommendations to help you with that.

With social media marketing, the key is to be consistent and limited. It is far more productive to be focused and committed to only two sites than to try to maintain many sites at once.

The key is to be consistent and limited.

But which two should we choose?

Your selection of two social media sites to maintain should depend on your book's message, audience type, and personal schedule. Here's a quick review (by no means exhaustive) of several social media sites to choose. Once you select two, it's time to do some deeper research about their functions and processes to see if it is truly right for you.

Twitter can be great for all authors but usually requires more time to keep it current. Tweets (messages) are limited to 280 characters, so comments are very short and laser to the point. This works best when an author consistently Tweets several times a day. Tweet-Tweet.

Facebook provides more of a variety and works best with a schedule for the different avenues of connection with your readers (advertising, posting, groups, etc.). Ad posting, short articles, snippets, and sharing quotes are often good ways to stay in touch with your audience on Facebook. It's probably best to select and limit your focus to a few types of activities to ensure adequate time for consistent, quality posts.

LinkedIn is something like Facebook, only focused on the business sector. It will probably work best if you have a business-oriented book. This requires a little more up-front study and time than the others for quality writing and material, but in this business sector it is worth it in the end.

YouTube is great for visually oriented authors and a book audience who loves personal stories. Creating a weekly video on YouTube about different subtopics of your book is a frequent marketing method used by independent authors. Google claims that you become more findable by literary agents and editors on YouTube. This typically requires up-front investment in a camera, tripod, and other equipment, but once you've got it, that's it.

Instagram seems to be more intense and personally engaging. It provides a variety of ways to connect and interact with a broader audience. Networking opportunities are available, and it even provides a way to monetize your writing, which provides an extra channel of income.

Snapchat seems to be the favored platform for younger millennials. If that's your audience, you will be actively posting friend-photos and videos to be viewed once, then they disappear. Public snapchats are only available for twenty-four hours, then they also disappear. Like other social media platforms, it requires constant attention to maintain ongoing effectiveness.

TikTok is the world's leading destination for short-form mobile videos. TikTok has 1 billion monthly active users and it is expected to hit 1.5 billion by the end of 2022. Before you ask, "Isn't that the dancing app for kids?." Oh no, it is much, much more. It's estimated that over 25% of all users are between the ages of 25-44. (Oberlo, 2023) TikTok is a great place to share your message and build your brand.

Google My Business is one of the most undiscovered marketing tactics for small businesses, including your book. You can post ads on Google My Business, like social media posts for free. Your Google My Business listing can drive traffic to your website or get your phone ringing.

Google is the most used search engine and is faster than any other host in the world. Your Google My Business listing is hosted by Google. Therefore, Google will find and show it faster than your website, Amazon listing, etc. I highly recommend you invest a little time building out your Google My Business listing.

Customize your content for each platform

When it comes to content and different platforms, it's not a one-size-fits-all situation we've got on our hands. You'll have to tailor your content to the different channels. This regards cover photos, video format and length, background music, theme, mood, and much more.

Learning which social media platforms work best for you and understanding how to best leverage them enables you to craft strategic and engaging content. To get the best results, test your content on different platforms.

Engage with your audience

Responding to your audience is the alpha and omega of growing your fan base. See your followers as relationships you need to maintain because people want to be seen and heard. Make it a habit to reply to comments and respond to messages as often as you can. Be human and, most importantly, be authentic, because people want to be able to relate to the influencers and channels they follow. Don't be afraid to show the real you.

Keep it simple

Always keep communication in every venue simple, free of industry jargon and academic mystery words. Experts are probably not reading your book. Your readers are the ones who are curious and don't already know about your subject and want to learn. When writing for any social media, be sure to include identifying information like the name of your book. That is forgotten more times than you can imagine.

Remember, active consistency is the key to making your social media efforts effective.

Create specific images or graphics

How many times have we heard the old saying, "A picture is worth a thousand words"? But it's true. Showing a picture always tells the story in less time and with greater impact.

Showing the picture always tells the story in less time and with greater impact.

Your audience will greatly appreciate good pictures, images, and graphics you've prepared for them. This will make your presentations far more engaging, interesting, and memorable.

Several free graphic programs online include Canva, Adobe Creative Cloud Express, Pablo by Buffer, Desygner, and Snappa. Take time to review the functions and processes of each one related to your selected social media platforms.

Spirit Media® ONE, our Gold level subscription, provides you the graphics and videos you need each month. And, our Platinum level subscription provides that PLUS we execute it all for you. Our Platinum level subscription is our most popular subscription. We all know we need to be marketing, but the truth is we don't want to keep up with it systematically. Spirit Media® to the rescue.

Use specific hashtags and use them smartly

Specific hashtags repetitively used can become familiar to your audience and that's a good thing. Some authors consider them essential for "findability."

What is a hashtag? They are keywords or phrases used in social media (typically tweets) with the # sign in front. Just make them up with two or three short key words.

Keep it all one single scrunch-word with no spaces. (Examples below.) A special feature of their uniqueness is that they become clickable links that reveal not only you and your brand, but everyone who uses that specific hashtag.

Hashtags become clickable links that reveal you and your brand.

Here are several popular author and writer hashtags to consider using for different reasons. If you find or compose a special hashtag that works especially well, please share it with us too.

#writerslife

#writerprobs

#writerproblems

#amwriting

#fantasywriter

#contemporarywriter

#WriteTip

#WritingPrompt

#BookGiveaway

#AskAgent

Conduct a quick search online and you'll likely find many other hashtags that could be particularly helpful to you.

Social media can be a powerful boost to your book sales, particularly on a continuing basis. But it takes constant tending, like a backyard garden, to produce profit effectively. It only works with consistent attention and nurture, so we highly recommend limiting your focus and time to two platforms.

Spirit Media® ONE allows you to post to ALL your social media sites simultaneously. You post one time and it goes to all your social media accounts. And, with our Platinum Subscription, we execute your social media for you.

The next secret to growing your book sales is like a sparkling gem in the middle of your jewelry collection. Strategically implemented, this strategy will broaden and deepen the scope and size of your book's advertising reach. It's time to learn how to take the simple steps to collect good book reviews.

Post consistently, but with purpose

Posting on social media is about consistency and value. If you're posting daily, but your audience doesn't find your content helpful, inspiring, or actionable, then they won't engage with or follow your accounts.

Using surveys and polls, ask customers what type of content they enjoy. This gives insight into what topics interest them, and even more importantly, what doesn't.

Look at analytics data to see what types of content perform best. Are people clicking on images? Videos? Links? Text only? What kind of content gets shared the most? How many likes does each piece receive? Which pieces generate the highest engagement?

Study each platform to see what types of content perform best on each.

Look at competitor activity to see what types of posts they share. Do they focus on product launches? Customer service updates? Sales promotions?

After finding content ideas, use a tool to automate your social media calendar, so you can schedule your content weeks or even months in advance. This can help you nail the right mix of content types and align with marketing themes, like upcoming campaigns.

Scheduling social media content that is intentional and driven by data and insights will pay off in attracting an authentic, engaged audience of social media followers.

Consider investing in paid social

It can be a really good investment to spend a bit of money on paid social promotions and advertisements. If done right, paid ads can not only grow your audience but also enhance the number of conversions while helping you target a greater number of people.

When choosing where to place your ads, it's helpful to know which networks are most popular within your target audience. Is it Facebook? TikTok? Instagram? It depends. There are also a number of different options on each platform. Stories, carousel, messenger, collection . . . That's why it's important to do your research before spending your dollars. With the right strategy and knowledge, there is a lot to be won through small measures. Don't forget to think about what you want to achieve with your campaign. Is it awareness? Do you want to drive traffic? Or are you looking for hard conversions? Make sure to measure the results so that you can optimize your efforts for the next time you want to invest a few bucks.

Create surveys and polls

Surveys and polls are a great way to both engage and activate your audience and a good trick to learn more about them. What do they like? What were their reactions to your latest campaign? What are their opinions on certain topics? If you want to know what your followers are thinking, just ask them.

Let us, once and for all, address the elephant in the room by providing a friendly reminder that it's never, ever, worth it to buy followers. This is a typical trap to fall into as these "followers" are likely bots or inactive accounts who won't engage with your content. It's also a false metric that might get you in trouble when it comes to collaborations and revenue.

It's also important to note that just because you have 5,000 Instagram followers doesn't automatically mean you're successful on social media. It might, but that's not the only metric you should pay attention to. Why? Some of these followers might not even check out your posts or links. The key to success is to build a community of loyal followers and fans who not only follow you but engage actively with your content and even share it with their own network. Most importantly, social media is a continually evolving landscape, so be ready to adapt your strategy at any time.

Host a competition

There are so many clever little ways to make it a win-win for you and your followers if you host a competition.

You could ask them to comment to take part in the competition, tag their friends or re-share your content, start a hashtag trend related to you or your products, or have them produce something in exchange for exposure or a prize. You grow your following and engage your audience at the same time as they get exposure and potential new followers or win a sweet prize.

Marketing is all about partnership. In the next chapter we will unpack your partnership with Amazon.

9

CHAPTER

Respect King Amazon

Today, Amazon is the No. 1 bookseller in the world. (Haines, 2021) If you are serious about selling your book then you will need to respect King Amazon.

Amazon makes publishing to the nations possible.

Amazon provides authors the opportunity to increase visibility, credibility, and sales to complete strangers in countries around the world. The more readers see and hear about your book, the more likely they will buy it over another book of the same subject.

Unfortunately, using Amazon is not easy.

It is no small tasks for every author in the world to learn everything they need to know about Amazon Kindle Direct Publishing (KDP), IngramSpark, Amazon Author Central, Amazon Seller Central, Findaway Voices in addition to ISBN, Library of Congress, US Copyright, Bookbaby, BookBub, Direct2Author, and everything else it takes just to publish a book.

One of the reasons I created Spirit Media® was to have a team that could help me as an author figure out Amazon. I knew that if Spirit Media® could help me we could help many authors around the world get their message to the nations.

At Spirit Media® we focus on four specific strategies for winning with Amazon:

1. Optimal Listings

2. Fulfilled by Amazon

3. Copyright and Trademark Infringement

4. Paid Ads on Amazon

Here are several important ingredients of building your book's visibility on Amazon.

Optimal Listing

The number one thing you can do to strengthen your presence on Amazon is to optimize your listing. Your listing either sells or fails. Sorry, there is no gray here. If your listing fails then the other three strategies will too.

2. Fulfilled by Amazon

3. Copyright and Trademark Infringement

4. Paid Ads on Amazon

It all starts with your 1. Optimal Listings. You will want to carefully build a strong Amazon book page for your book.

Your Amazon book page is important for authors because it's the first thing readers will see when clicking on your book from a list of publications with similar subject titles.

Starting on the left of the author page, the reader will immediately see a picture of your book with the cover graphics, the title, and your author name.

Treat Your Cover and Title as Sales Tools.

In Chapter One we discussed the vital first impression leading to a book sale is the book cover and title. Let's take a deeper dive into the marketing impact of the cover and title.

Professional marketers claim that the cover and title are at least 50% of the cause of a sale. There's a 50/50 chance it catches a reader's attention, or not.

Your book's cover has less than five seconds to draw in a potential reader.

A beautiful ornate cover design with a simple title will often undermine sales. But a cover specially designed to be both cleanly attractive and draw the reader in with a bold title will produce many more sales.

Be bold. Just presenting the subject is simply not enough in today's market. So, you ask, how do I do that?

Right now, in your mind, picture two books displayed on the Amazon book selection site. The book cover on the left has ornate artistic graphics surrounding the simple title, Breakfast Nutrition.

The second book's content presents the same subject, breakfast nutrition. The difference is, it has a clean and clear design background with this title: What Never-Ever to Eat for Breakfast

Q: Why does the second book get many, many more clicks?

A: The first title simply provides the subject, without any zing or punch. It desperately needs to sizzle.

The second book title boldly promises to reveal information the reader probably doesn't know. It teases curiosity. It promises both nutrition and little-known information. The reader's mind immediately asks, "Whaaat is it . . . I should NOT be eating for breakfast?" and they psychologically want to know more. That bold benefit title with a cleanly designed background will produce many more clicks and sales compared to the first one.

Marketing your book successfully requires a clean design and benefit-oriented title with punch.

Make sure to always answer the question readers are asking: why should I read your book? Many book titles focus on what the book is about.

Buyers buy "why" not "what."

Tell buyers why they need your book. Always answer the question, "what is this book about?" or "what's in it for me?" by answering why readers should read this book.

It is essential to treat your cover design and title as sales tools.

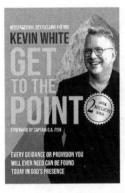

Kevin White

Get to the Point: Every Guidance or Provision You Will Ever Need Can Be Found Today in God's Presence

^ See less

★★★★★ (60)

The demographics information showing with your book picture appears based upon the setup process forms you completed in advance.

Once potential buyers make it through your cover the next important part of this page is the book description and details about the book.

At Spirit Media®, our Editor team and Amazon team work tirelessly to identify

what we call the Marketing Strengths for each book we publish.

Our Marketing Strengths section answers these questions:

1. What category will this book be listed under (KDP Category Finder Tool)?

2. What is this book about (25 words)?

3. Who is this book for?

4. What are some ideas about the target audience or market of the book so we can generate keywords?

5. Keywords (rated by Google Ads Keyword Planner)?

6. Book Description - Short Version (300 words for back of the book)?

7. Book Description - Long Version (for Amazon)?

8. Author Bio - Short Version (300 words for back of the book)?

9. Author Bio - Long Version (for Amazon)?

Identifying the book's keywords is very important. Here is a sample list of keywords for this book - *Spirit Media's ULTIMATE Book Marketing Guide*:

GOOGLE KEYWORDS

Keywords	Average Monthly Searches	Keywords	Average Monthly Searches
YouTube	185,000,000	Advertisement	74,000
Amazon	124,000,000	Authors	60,500
Google	68,000,000	Editing	60,500
Market	1,500,000	Guide	49,500
Book	550,000	eBook	49,500
Entrepreneur	368,000	Promotion	40,500
Success	201,000	Generosity	40,500
Guarantee	165,000	Publishing	33,100
Graphic Design	165,000	Book Cover	33,100
International	165,000	Awareness	27,100
Sales	165,000	Websites	22,200
Writers	135,000	PPC	22,200
Audiobook	135,000	Worldwide	22,200
Global	135,000	Bestseller	14,800
Marketing	110,000	Paperback	9,900
Strategies	110,000	Self-Publishing	5,400
Media	110,000	Bestselling	4,400
Tactics	90,500	Solopreneur	2,900
Branding	90,500	Paid Ads	1,600
Failure	90,500	Hardback	880

 AMAZON KEYWORDS

Keywords	Average Monthly Searches	Keywords	Average Monthly Searches
amazon	242,072	awareness	635
youtube	179,338	bestseller	596
google	60,082	entrepreneur	539
book	7,155	paperback	364
sales	4,836	writers	247
ebook	4,829	generosity	234
cover	4,590	guide	231
design	2,581	editing	202
audiobook	2,041	authors	162
marketing	1,966	failure	141
international	795	bestselling	129
media	1,296	solopreneur	121
graphic	1,012	worldwide	108
global	941	websites	101
tactics	939	success	86
market	939	publishing	77
branding	716	hardback	28
promotion	714	ppc	12

The goal is to identify the top 10-12 keywords and then intentionally and tastefully embed them in the title, subtitle, book description, and author bio. Other important but secondary keywords can be intentionally embedded into the introduction, chapter titles, and conclusion. By intentional I don't mean obnoxiously, but tastefully.

As you can see, we have intentionally sprinkled keywords from our lists all throughout this book.

Every author in the world who's writing a book needs to find this book.

Keywords help accomplish this.

Target Your Readers with Categories and Keywords (Metadata)

Metadata is the information you provide about the book's content. It is the most important factor for the reader's search box optimization. It helps readers find and discover your content more easily.

The metadata (book's keywords) should be targeted for the readers. Again, be careful to include keywords that are relevant to your target audience and describe what your content is about in a concise way. As described above, meta descriptions of your book content on the book page should be written in a way that will make potential readers want to click on it. This is assuming you are intent on selling more books.

Utilize Amazon's KDP Select Program

Amazon's KDP Select program provides many benefits including free enrollment and special Kindle promotional tools. Being a KDP select author means readers will have access to borrow your book (something like an online library) which gives your book amazing extra exposure. Another benefit of KDP Select is the ability to run price promotions. Note: when enrolling in KDP select, Amazon requires an immediate exclusive sales right for a ninety-day period. After that, you can market your book anywhere on any site in the world.

Customize Your Amazon Author Page

Your readers need to see who you are, your expertise, and be initially impressed with your ability to offer real solutions. First impressions are lasting impressions, so work hard to make it really good. When composing your author bio section, add a personal tone to your description. This helps them connect and feel drawn to pursue your book one step further.

Little known secret sales strategy: you can include an incentive in your author bio. This could help you build a powerful customer list straight from Amazon.

Before the Release Date, Set Up Pre-Orders.

Authors typically sell books through Kindle before they're published, allowing readers to pre-order the book. Pre-ordering is definitely a beneficial marketing strategy for several important reasons. Increasing immediate sales and expanding visibility toward your launch date are only two of them.

You might consider pre-order BOGO deals, or special pricing to encourage presales. These often provide significant bumps toward pushing your book higher on the closely watched pre-release sales report lists.

The stronger your pre-order sales become, the more buzz-buzz-buzz is generated about its upcoming release. This becomes increasingly attractive to retailers. They are keenly aware that big pre-sales numbers can influence a book's discoverability, which makes it more likely to show up on the top of a bestseller list once released. Dollar signs start pulsating and flashing green in their eyes, driving them crazy.

It is important to understand that pre-order listings can only be revised once. No changes shall be made after the second upload; otherwise the author will be banned on setting up pre-orders in the future. Also, updates on manuscript shall be made two weeks prior to launch. There is a ton of technology behind Amazon so you want

to make sure your files are perfect before uploading them to KDP.

Fulfilled by Amazon

Once your book is published, you'll want to order several hundred print copies and get them loaded up with Fulfilled by Amazon. There is a registration process to set this up. It can be complicated. Spirit Media® handles this for our authors. This is where your book is stocked in Amazon fulfillment centers to be sold by Amazon including Amazon Prime. Amazon charges small fees to warehouse your books. Amazon deducts a flat fee to fulfill orders every time someone orders your book. Through Fulfilled by Amazon you're engaging Amazon to distribute your book. This incentivizes Amazon to help you sell your book.

Print Copies

As a full service publisher and marketing company, Spirit Media® offers the lowest printing costs anywhere.

Print on Demand of paperback and hardback is a viable option for some quantities below 1,000 copies. The benefit of this is fair price and quick turn around without having to invest thousands of dollars to mass produce copies of your book. The hardback version of print on demand is a case cover identical to the paperback except on hardback material. This technology is faster for print on demand but is also more expensive per piece than the traditional cloth stitched hardback cover with dust jacket which is available through large print houses.

For larger orders of 1,000 copies and above, digital or offset bulk printing offers better prices. This is where you get the traditional cloth stitched hardback cover with dust jacket. The turn around for bulk printing can be 6-8 weeks. Orders start at 1,000+. Orders can be split between paperback and hardback. For example one order of 2,500 copies can consist of 2,000 paperbacks and 500 hardbacks. Orders this size can bring the cost per piece down significantly from Print on Demand prices.

Copyright and Trademark Infringement

The ideal goal is for your Amazon listing to show that your book is sold by Fulfilled by Amazon and no other sellers. Unfortunately, the better your book sells the more attractive it is for 3rd party distributors to start selling your book. We call these companies hijackers and pirates. In order to compete they offer your book at cheaper prices. All they need to do is collect fifty cents from millions of books and they make good money. This drives your prices down which means fewer royalties for you.

When this happens (and it will) you then need to file cases with Amazon to prove the book is yours and the pirates are not legally authorized to sell your book. This now becomes copyright and trademark infringement. Unfortunately, Amazon does not make this easy. Amazon gets paid the same whether the copy sold is legal or illegal. It takes weeks of cease and desist orders to enforce copyright and trademark protection. Spirit Media® is a registered trademark on Amazon so that we can protect our authors from copyright infringement.

Paid Ads on Amazon

The difference between selling fifty copies and 5,000 copies on Amazon is paid ads on Amazon. These ads are called PPC ads for Pay Per Click ads. Using your keywords you now build and launch ad campaigns to show your book to potential buyers. If you've used Amazon at all you've seen "sponsored" products. These are paid ads. It brings your book listing up higher. If a potential buyer clicks on your ad then Amazon assesses a small fee for pay per click.

The risk is Amazon gets paid whether the buyer buys your book or not. That is why optimizing your listing is so important. If PPC is not effective either the ad campaign is weak or the book listing is weak. It is important that both be maximized to work in partnership together toward selling your book.

As a full service publisher and marketing company, Spirit Media® partners with our authors to handle this for them. While this isn't free it is more effective than doing it yourself. We have paid professionals on our team that do nothing but make paid ads on Amazon effective. As a publisher we are highly motivated to get your books selling. The last thing we ever want to do is just put another book on the market.

At Spirit Media® we exist to turn writers into international bestselling authors. We believe the message of God through the people of God is worthy to be taken to the nations. That's all 195 nations of the world. While Amazon doesn't offer worldwide domination (yet), Amazon is the number one book seller in the world. The way to the top is through Amazon. Let Spirit Media® partner with you to make that happen for your book.

In the next chapter, we will discuss additional paid ads that can accelerate your book sales.

CHAPTER

Using Paid Ads

In addition to Amazon PPC you can also promote your books using other paid ads like:

- Google
- Bing (Microsoft)
- Facebook
- Instagram
- LinkedIn
- Twitter

The goal of an advertising strategy is to create a map that produces the best path toward book profits. Book marketing and promotion can get a bit challenging, but, clear, realistic, and measurable steps, attentively followed, greatly increase the chance of success.

Use paid ads to increase the probability of sales and success.

The following steps for a book advertising campaign are proven to produce measurable, positive results for many book sales campaigns.

Google

Run Ads on Google

Note: Google's policy restricts ads for eBooks but allows ads for paperback, hardback, and audiobooks.

Google can be tricky and expensive if you don't know what you're doing. I certainly didn't. Most authors and business owners don't.

Welcome to Death Valley

The challenge is, in general, ALL paid ads expose the Death Valley between marketing and tech.

A tech expert can understand everything about the technical side of the platform, but completely fail to produce successful ads because they do not understand marketing.

By the technical side of paid ads, I mean understanding the following:

- Google AdWords

  (now called simply Google Ads)
- ad campaigns
- ad groups
- ad rank
- quality score
- long-tail keywords
- keyword competition
- maximum bid and bid position
- click-through rates (CTR)
- relevant keywords
- conversion tracking
- Google Analytics code
- A/B testing
- ad extensions
- quality score

A marketing person can understand everything about marketing, but totally fail to produce successful ads because they do not understand the technical requirements of the platform.

By the marketing side of paid ads, I mean understanding the following:

- digital ads
- display ads
- target audience
- demographics
- advertising budget
- sales copy
- keywords
- positive keywords
- negative keywords
- headlines

- descriptions

- graphics

- call to action

- mobile friendly

- landing pages

- return on investment (ROI)

Finding someone who is proficient at both is like finding a needle in a haystack. Good luck.

One of our first hires when starting Spirit Media® was a Google Ads expert. We intentionally hired someone with a basic understanding and without much experience. She had passion and determination. I knew that if she could learn the technical side I could offer the marketing side. Our manager knew enough to point her in the right direction. She camped out on Google for several weeks and soon passed Google's certifications. Within a few months she had us humming. She and our team learned the technical side. I was able to guide the marketing side.

Success with paid ads happens when technical and marketing come together.

Whether it is Amazon, Google, Facebook, or any platform, one of the most tedious tasks is identifying the decisions to be made in plain English.

It helped us to create what we call our Paid Ad Fact Sheet. We now do this for every ad campaign we run, whether it is Amazon, Google, or Facebook. They are not all the same, but they identify the decisions and the answers for the ad. For example:

- screenshot of the ad

- graphic

- headline

- description

- geographic location

- daily budget

- results

- reach

- amount spent

- click-through rate (CTR)

- clicks

- frequency

- suggestions for improvements

We made this information clear so that our clients can follow the rationale. Now that's pure gold.

The more we bring technical and marketing together in everyday, plain English, the greater our success.

Years ago, I would beat my head against the wall because I'd work with techies who would talk geek and totally stall the conversation. It wasn't until Spirit Media® hired and trained our own techies that we won this battle. Everyone on our staff knows we are a marketing-first company. Our Paid Ad Team learned the technical side of paid ads in order to succeed at marketing.

You Can Do It.

Get this right and you too can be successful with paid ads. While success with paid ads depends on bringing tech and marketing together, you must commit to marketing first. All the technology in the world is of little value if marketing is not present. Make sure the tech side is driven by marketing, and it will be successful.

Personally, I decided not to dive into the technical side. That is not my gift. As a published author, I gladly hire Spirit Media® to take care of my paid ads. I recommend Spirit Media® to you too. Regardless, I'm laying out the tactics in this book that are guaranteed to increase sales of your book.

While paid ads are complex, they are absolutely necessary if you want to go from ten books a month to 500 books a month. The difference is paid ads. So here is what you have to know . . .

In addition to connecting tech and marketing, you should:

1. **Start slowly**. Prove you have a successful ad, then increase the budget.

2. **Follow the math**. If you're too busy to follow the math then pause the ad, otherwise, you could spend a great deal of money without attaining success.

3. **Set your budget**. Know how much you are spending and have realistic expectations.

4. **Optimize your book listing**, website, or landing page. Successful ads drive

traffic to your book. If it is not ready to sell, then you're going to waste money.

5. **Pay attention.** Monitor the ad. If you see impressions but not clicks, something is wrong. If you see clicks but not sales, then something is wrong. Find out what it is and fix it.

6. **Repeat 1-5 constantly.**

One wrong keyword could show your ad to people who do not care about your book. If you're selling a cookbook and use the keyword "pizza," your ad could be showing up for people trying to order a pizza for dinner—people who care nothing about buying a cookbook. If so, fix it. Remove the keyword "pizza."

Stay focused on marketing and you'll figure out the tech side of paid ads, otherwise, call Spirit Media® and we will gladly handle paid ads for you.

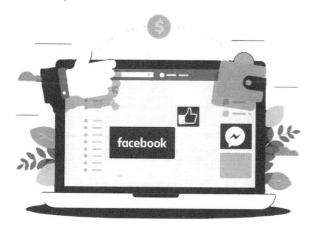

Run Ads on Facebook

Facebook has its own unique methods of advertising strategies and plans to increase the chance of your book "selling-like-crazy."

Again, it takes a learning curve commitment, but it's one that has proven well worth it for many new authors.

There are many testimonials of authors creeping along at $50 a month in sales before they finally invested in Facebook ads. The investment increased their book's exposure and rocketed their sales into thousands of dollars per month.

Facebook heavily promotes its audience, targeting techniques to build engaging ads that produce more attention and sales.

When it comes to paid ads, focus first on Amazon, Google, and Facebook. Once you're ready, then consider: Bing (Microsoft), Instagram, LinkedIn, and Twitter. While each platform is different, you will see that the principles are the same.

Select the Right Keywords.

The No. 1 biggest contribution from the marketing side of paid ads is keywords. The whole point is to get into the minds of potential buyers. What are they typing into their search browsers?

Keep Marketing First.

Remember to approach your paid ads with marketing first, and you'll find success. Sorry techies. If you're a techie, God bless you. We can't do our marketing without you.

In this next chapter, we give techies a break and things get much easier as we discuss getting book reviews.

11

CHAPTER

Collect Book Reviews

Social proof that a book is worth buying comes from reviews. Amazon marketers know that editorial reviews from experts produce more sales. For this reason, they place them higher up on an Amazon product page than customer reviews. But both are important.

It has been proven that a majority of readers rely on the editorial and customer reviews mostly when looking for a new author. If many of the readers report disappointment, that kills sales clicks.

In general, according to Dixa Research. . .

93% of customers will read online reviews.

While 47% of those customers say they usually talk with others about a positive experience, a whopping 95% share negative experiences.

That gives extra impetus to your launch team activities. Continually monitoring editorial and customer reviews, especially in Amazon, is vital to the robust health of your book sales.

But don't forget to have your team obtain editorial reviews—since they are the ones most read and followed.

Opening your connection with Amazon is an important part of your book's marketing strategy. It may provide more than 50% of your future sales.

As authors, we want to get our books in front of as many potential readers as possible. One of the most effective ways of doing that is to acquire reviews from authors, reviewers, bloggers, and other professionals in the publishing industry. Not only does this provide legitimacy to our message, but it helps get our books in front of totally new audiences.

Before securing book reviews

Public relations professionals make a big deal about advance preparation before you're interviewed for your book. They recommend that authors write out a short explanation of the problem the book identifies, then clearly write several solutions presented.

You, the author, are the expert on this subject, so communicating with passion, clarity, and deep sincerity is paramount to your potential client's first impression. Keep in mind that one book review can catch other high-profile interviews that could put

your book on the bestseller list. Excellent preparation will be a vital key to making that happen.

Write a short explanation of the problem the book identifies . . . with several solutions.

Network with other authors

There are a few different ways to network with other authors, peers, and mentors. These include attending publishing conferences, local writing workshops, general events, educational conferences, and social media groups. Basically, include any gathering of people (large or small) that might be interested in your topic.

When networking at an event, it is best to diligently pursue inspiration and feedback. Building relationships with book bloggers and reviewers will produce reviews of your book. Always go with lots of business cards and books in the car.

COLLECT BOOK REVIEWS.

The wisdom of Proverbs tells us, "He who earnestly seeks good finds favor" (11:27, NKJV). And favor produces special reviews of your book. Just one interesting review from one key contact can rocket your book sales to Mars.

Get early customer reviews

Reach out to your readers to see if anyone is interested in receiving an Advanced Reader Copy (ARC). Then, on the release day, encourage them to give you an honest review. This is a great way to boost interest and build buzz for your book. It also may help identify areas that need improvement before the book goes to print.

When selecting reviewers, target individuals with special personal reasons to be favorable to your topic.

Reach out to bloggers and other influencers who have a large following. Sometimes offering incentives, such as giving away free copies or offering a discount on the purchase price, is effective.

Another possibility is to post your book on Amazon's Kindle Preview program, which allows potential readers to read up to 10% of your book for free. Keep in mind, though, these early reviews can be mixed. Some people may love your book, while others not so much. So, it's important to be strategic about distributing early copies.

Are book reviews important to an effective marketing strategy? Absolutely. By carefully managing early book reviews, your book gets a tremendous boost before it's even available to the general public.

Next, are you ready for this? Here's an awesome BIG list of the best book review and promotion sites for your book marketing campaigns. Not only can you collect a lot of positive reviews but you can gain amazing exposure to publishers, retailers, and new reading audiences.

This is an awesome list to choose from.

THE BEST BOOK REVIEW SITES

To save you time and money our team has prepared a list of the BEST book review sites. Please email us at editor@spiritmedia.us if you have additional recommendations.

Goodreads

 goodreads.com

The Goodreads.com website provides book recommendations. With over 125 million members and 3.5 billion (with a B) books, it boasts being the largest site for readers and book recommendations in the world.

It's free to join and free to promote your book. You can connect your blog, advertise, and take full advantage of their Author Program (AP). The AP gives you access to key marketing tools that help you build a buzz of conversations around your book. Check out their advertising plans at https://www.goodreads.com/advertisers. A special promotional giveaway program on the site is available to US and Canadian customers.

Finally, Goodreads.com has a great Authors & Advertisers Blog with a constant flow of valuable information and tips on how to market your book and how to maximize their author's program to your benefit. https://www.goodreads.com/news?content_type=author_blogs

LibraryThing

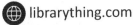 librarything.com

Here's another huge site worth your attention. LibraryThing is an online book club boasting 2.3 million members and claiming to be the largest book club in the world.

Their free online database allows you to create and organize an inventory of all your books.

An additional attraction drawing readers to this site is social networking that connects people based on the books they share. A powerful added feature for authors includes the Early Reviewer Program. This allows

you, the author, to give out free copies in exchange for a reader's honest review, often creating a super-added boost to the conversation buzz around your new book.

Kirkus Reviews

 kirkusreviews.com

Here is a leading journal of pre-publication reviews in the USA where publishers and retailers frequently find new books. To keep their business alive, they are always looking for books that will sell. Your book could be next, with a good review on Kirkus Reviews.

You can promote your book here by emailing bookmarketing@kirkus.com to schedule a call and discuss book campaign options and pricing details. If you select this book campaign method, there will be promotions in both the Kirkus Reviews magazine and their high-circulation email newsletter. With so much commercial and individual focus on Kirkus reviews, it may be a very profitable campaign selection for you.

Clarion Review

 publishers.forewordreviews.com

Clarion Review is a source for an independent author to obtain a 450-word professional critique of all aspects of their book. The Clarion Review fee is $499 per book for express critiques of 4-6 weeks. If you select this method, your book review will be posted on their high traffic website for maximum exposure. Licensed book wholesalers around the US and Canada, their partners, such as Ingram, Baker & Taylor, Cengage, and Bowker will spread the word to many thousands of librarians and booksellers. Added benefit: their review lends strong credibility to both your book and to you as a published author.

Foreword Indie Reviews

 publishers.forewordreviews.com

As a sister company of Clarion Reviews, Foreword Reviews Magazine also conducts professional critiques of new publications, at no cost. However, their program is a bit different, requiring receipt of the new book (printed or digital) in their offices at least four months in advance of publication. They also offer different attractive advertising options for new authors, including website advertising (sidebar ads for $18) and email advertising ($250 -$400). A special attraction that receives extra attention to both sales professionals and retail sellers is a book award site. https://publishers.forewordreviews.com/awards/#why-register.

Readers' Favorite

 readersfavorite.com

Another very popular book review company is Readers' Favorite. With a free review option, breadth of subject genres, publisher's participation list, and many awards from the Association of Independent Authors, Readers' Favorite is truly a favorite, becoming the fastest growing book review and award contest site.

Free reviews take 10-12 weeks and single express reviews for $59 can be scheduled for completion in two weeks. For a fee of $129 they will complete three express reviews (2-3 weeks completion), and $199 for five express reviews, also completed in 2-3 weeks.

When using their services, your book review will be posted on their site, KOBO, Google Books, Facebook, Twitter, Instagram and Pinterest. An added key benefit is that their reviewers often post reviews to their blogs and social media sites, greatly increasing your book's exposure. Your review will also be indexed by search engines like Google, which recognizes and formats them with their starred rating, just like Amazon and Goodreads. Finally, if your book earns a coveted five-star review, they award you a free "Five Star" digital seal for your website and a high-resolution version for your book cover. Yes, that seal brings more valuable attention from the whole book publishers' industry, greatly impacting your sales figures.

Reader Views

 readerviews.com

Reader Views is another popular book review and book awards site. They offer a free standard review service, but be cautious because they do not guarantee a favorable review. Their paid review services range from $139 to $529 and they can be reached at https://www.readerviews.com/publicitycampaigns/. You may also find their book giveaway program interesting for your book sales campaign.

Book List

 booklistonline.com

This is the official review publication of the American Library Association. They accept books to review and produce reports both online and in print. You can connect with them at https://www.booklistonline.com/get-reviewed.

Believe it or not, the American Library Association also offers advertising options ranging from $1,000 to $1,500. Learn all about it at https://drive.google.com/file/d/1z4iKd6-S_woO_GEGkrmFiS4H5f3k4phK/view.

BlueInk Review

 blueinkreview.com

Self-published authors from a wide variety of genres love this premier source for professional book reviews. BlueInk Review is connected with other indie book review companies like Goodreads and huge retail book companies like Barnes & Noble, as well. Paid book review packages start from $395 to $695 (https://www.blueinkreview.com/purchase/).

A "starred" book review from BlueInk Review is a definite plus for your book marketing and sales. To enhance your marketing strategy, BlueInk Review also offers purchase of their book seals.

Rain Taxi Review of Books

 raintaxi.com

Publishers or authors desiring review of a new book may submit printed copies only to the Rain Taxi company mailing address, PO Box 3840, Minneapolis, MN 55403. Only printed books or bound galleys are accepted for consideration. Electronic files of any kind are not accepted.

Their review genres are mostly limited to poetry, fiction, literary nonfiction, art, and graphic novels. Connect with them in advance if you are seeking a review of a children's or young adult book, audio book, or chapbook.

Rain Taxi completes new release reviews for free and they have advertising on their website available for authors' marketing campaigns.

Book Life

 booklife.com

Book Life website is by Publishers Weekly and is dedicated to independent authors. They offer both free reviews and more extensive professional paid reviews (guaranteed for $399). Delivery of the review takes six weeks, unless the author requests an expedited process for an additional $100 fee. The paid option includes your review appearing in the Book Life section of Publishers Weekly.

If you choose this option to help market your book, please note that you'll need to create a Book Life account first to submit a book for review.

BookBub

 bookbub.com

BookBub provides a free signup to submit a book and use most of their services. It's known as a free service for millions of readers to discover books they love. This provides an open door for publishers and authors to drive sales and find new fans. Some of the ways BookBub helps you reach a host of readers is via featured deals, promoting your discounted book, new release alerts, and author profiles. Check out their website for more. Note that the cost will vary depending on your book price. Go to https://www.bookbub.com/partners/pricing.

IndieReader

 indiereader.com

With more than 10,000 subscribers, the goal of IndiReader is to obtain honest and positive reviews that will empower your book sales. They not only utilize verified reader and independent author reviews, but include a team of editors, librarians, and journalists, as well. IndiReader will give your book visibility.

A customary review takes 7-9 weeks for $275. If you want it in a rush, it costs $350 with a 4-6 week turnaround.

BookViral

 bookviralreviews.com

BookViral's mission is to discover new and talented authors. They provide professional reviews in all fiction and most non-fiction genres, including poetry. BookViral started as a book review club and is now one of the biggest book review sites.

To assist authors' discoverability and increase their book sales, BookViral also offers a full list of author services, including editing, website design, and SEO book advertising.

The US Review of Books

 theusreview.com

The US Review of Books is a Hoffer Award site providing professional book reviews for all publishers and independent authors within a very long list of fiction and non-fiction genres. With over 20K subscribers who receive a monthly newsletter with book reviews, they are highly respected and known as a leading book review organization. Services range from $99 to $249 per book depending on delivery time requested.

Reading Deals

 readingdeals.com

Reading Deals is a book promotion service that finds bargain and free book deals and promotes them to their readers, for free. Authors seeking to increase exposure for their books can submit for free or select a guaranteed submission for only $29.

The added benefit to you is that readers who pick your book must agree to leave a review on Amazon in return. When a customer discovers a longer list of reviews on Amazon, they know your book is being purchased. Hopefully, most of the reviews will give your book a high rating.

The Review Crew & Three Nice Mice Book Blog

 cozymysteryreview.wixsite.com

Well. At least this isn't the famous "Three Blind Mice". These Three-Nice-Mice are a group of reliable reviewers from the Review Crew eager to read and review for you. They also assist authors with shipping and mailing list services. Check them out to discover what they mean by "other functionalities."

If you can pay using Zelle, the Review Crew charges $18 for their service for up to ten copies of your eBook. For hard copies, the fee is $16 for up to ten copies. If you are unable to use Zelle, the charge is $23 for eBooks and $21 for hard copies: https://cozymysteryreview.wixsite.com/home/author-faq

Joelbooks

 joelbooks.com

Joelbooks is a great site offering a variety of essential marketing services for authors/publishers. The costs vary on the type of service, the level, expected deadlines, and selected deal.

Joelbooks has also partnered with BooksGoSocial to offer a discounted solution to get your book on Netgalley. NetGalley+ from BooksGoSocial is the low-cost way for any author or publisher to join NetGalley, the No. 1 service in the world for getting honest, valuable reader reviewers on Amazon: https://bgsauthors.com/product/products/netgalleyservice/

Discounted packages at Joelbooks start at $79 for one-month's listing, but note that this option isn't available at the Netgalley site. Because of their partnership, you can secure a 50% discount as a self-publisher.

Ereader News Today

 ereadernewstoday.com

Ereader News Today makes available bargain and free ebooks in a reader's chosen genre, every day. How does this benefit you, the author? Submitting your book will open the door to a whole new population of readers. This can be an important part of your marketing promotion strategy to drive your book into the bestseller lists.

Your book will be sent out to over 475,000 Facebook fans and 200,000 email subscribers who are avid ebook readers. The standard fee is $60 for books priced below $2.99, and $150 for books priced $2.99 and above.

Fussy Librarian

 authors.thefussylibrarian.com

The Fussy Librarian is an email list service with 565,000 readers that matches the reader to their specific genre of book.

Your book will be promoted on their website for each day of a giveaway, and in their free subscriber's newsletter by genre, title, one-sentence description and a link to retailers. Check their authors' site for policies, procedures, and costs.

COLLECT BOOK REVIEWS.

Freebooksy

 freebooksy.com

Freebooksy finds available free eBooks every day, mostly on Amazon Kindle. Subscribers sign up to receive a daily email with a list of free eBooks available according to their selected genre.

Authors pay a fee of $75 to list their book. The benefit is receiving added reviews that promote and increase book sales. Though author reviews are mixed, some authors have reported a very positive increase in reviews and sales using Freebooksy.

Bargain Booksy

 bargainbooksy.com

Bargain Books is a sister site of Freebooksy that promotes your book for free if it's priced between 99 cents and $4.99. It does not feature or promote free books to its readers in its daily email and website. A free author submission for review is available, yet, due to its huge popularity, only about 5% of submissions receive exposure. But, no surprise, there is a purchase option available that reserves a slot for your title.

ManyBooks

 manybooks.net

ManyBooks provides professional, in-depth feedback on your book for a fee starting at $79 with a four-week turnaround. If your book scores a four- to five-star rating, it is included in their "Book of the Month" list, and they provide editorial quotes valuable for your website, Amazon page, advertising, book cover, and promotions.

BKnights

 fiverr.com

BKnights can only be found on a writer's job service board at fiverr.com. They claim to be a number one publishing service for independent authors, with networks and contacts throughout the world. They also claim their publishing platform can reach over 15,000 readers. We cannot verify those claims.

DigitalBookSpot

 digitalbookspot.com

DigitalBookSpot claims to be an international book promoter, and affiliate of Amazon Kindle. If you are offering your book for free as a promotion they will promote your book for $5 to their book audience. They claim to have thousands of readers with lots of positive reviews and a big FaceBook fanbase.

RobinReads

 robinreads.com

RobinReads only promotes to its 194,000 members books priced at 99 cents or less. All author submissions must have an ASIN, sufficient professional reviews, and pass their review selection process. Only 10% of requests are accepted. They charge $60 to promote nonfiction.

Hidden Gems

 hiddengemsbooks.com

The most effective review service in the business by a large margin, they generate a ton of quality reviews where the reviewers clearly have read the books and would post multiple paragraph reviews. They even send you a follow-up email with selected additional comments from their ARC list. The only problem with Hidden Gems is the booking time, which extends to half a year or longer for most genres.

Booktubes - YouTube has interesting video channels with book-nerds reviewing and discussing books. Here's a list of a few of the best YouTube channels about books:

Rincey Reads

 youtube.com/c/rinceyreads

Rincey claims to have 30.4K subscribers to her book review video channel. Check her out.

Little Book Owl

 youtube.com/c/LittleBookOwl

This little lady claims to have 180K subscribers. Actually, you will find an impressive number of book reviews on her site. She discusses non-fiction, science fiction, and contemporary books, among many more.

Better Than Food - 142K subscribers

 youtube.com/c/
BetterThanFoodBookReviews

We think that only a total book-nerd showing a picture of himself eating a printed page from a book would say that books are better than food. However, his video book review channel includes a good variety of fiction and non-fiction, along with other genres. Take a look. Maybe you can get him to read and review your book . . . if you present it as a tasty bite.

SITES NOT RECOMMENDED

Based on our careful reviews we highly recommend caution and careful consideration before using the following sites. We cannot recommend them.

- US Book fairs by Bowker and Combined Book Exhibit

- Bowker Services (for book marketing)

- ScoreIt.

- Reedsy Discovery

Securing book reviews from multiple sites included in our comprehensive list above will definitely boost exposure and increase sales results. Depending on the tightness of your schedule, consistently Include one more review at consistent intervals (once a week, once every two weeks, etc.). Increased exposure makes it easier to secure other reviews and, bottom line, increases sales more and more.

Is there another strategy that helps an independent author like you to move the sales train forward? Oh yes, there is. In the next chapter we introduce you to the exciting subject of how to win book awards.

CHAPTER

Book Awards

Book awards are another opportunity to get people talking about your book.

What is the benefit? Being listed on a winning books list provides amazing exposure to publishers, retailers, and new reading audiences.

When entering and winning an award, you will want to shout it out on your website, in your advertising, and on your social media posts. It's a particularly potent strategy to make an award-winning or special publicity event happen every sixty days to brag to the world.

The goal of marketing is to get people talking.

In an effort to save you time and money, our team of expert marketing professionals have compiled the following awesome list of the BEST book award sites for you. You will enjoy this list.

INDEPENDENT AUTHOR BOOK AWARD SITES

Page Turners Award

 pageturnerawards.com

This award is sponsored, based, and registered in the UK but is open to any authors, writers, and screenwriters worldwide. Book Award categories include best cover, best series, best genre, best co-authored book, and best golden author (60+). The fee to enter is £30.

Reader's Favorite

 readersfavorite.com

Registered authors are automatically entered to win one of more than 260 prizes worth a combined total of $100,000, just by having an entry. Benefits for the author include free and paid book reviews, helpful articles and writing services, and significant exposure to the retail book publishing industry. For the reader, there are more than 150 genres of books to choose from.

The National Indie Excellence Awards

 indieexcellence.com

The extra prestige of these awards come from the fact that they are highly selective, with only one winner per category. Winners and finalists of The National Indie Excellence Awards receive all the promotion and industry exposure that comes with other book awards. The author fee is $75 per entry/per category.

The Foreword INDIES Book of the Year Awards

 publishers.forewordreviews.com

Winning an award from this organization for independent authors brings a cash prize along with significant international attention and buzz from booksellers, librarians, and publishing professionals. Entering your book to be considered in their awards programs also buys a subscription to their magazine, Foreword Reviews. The entry fee depends on the date and category and it ranges from $79 to $99.

Book Excellence Award

 bookexcellenceawards.com

This is an international book awards competition open to indie and traditional publishers alike. Prize packages are valued up to $4,000 and the entry fee is $149 for each category. Just by entering, you receive all-access to their book marketing course, valued at $500.

Reader Views

 readerviews.com

All author entries receive a review and promotion on Reader Views' website, social media, and other platforms. Your book is listed on Goodreads, BookBub, and in their newsletter. They also give extra exposure to your book on their website and blogs. All entries are eligible for one of their grand prizes totaling $2,500 cash. The entry fee is $89 to $99.

The Benjamin Franklin Book Awards (IBPA)

 ibpabenjaminfranklinaward.com

Winners receive recognition on all Independent Book Publishers Association (IBPA) social media and their website. The company also provides promotion to trade journals and libraries, among other great marketing perks. The author entry fee is $229 ($95 for IBPA members).

American Book Fest "Best Book" Award

 americanbookfest.com

American Book Fest book awards are designed explicitly to garner promotion that equals media attention and book sales in the publishing and entertainment world. Author entries are $69 per title/per category.

Shelf Unbound Best Indie Book Competition

 shelfmediagroup.com

Winners are given editorial coverage in the December/January Shelf Unbound magazine, as well as a year of full page ads in the publication. They do not accept children's picture books for entry. Author entry fees are $100 per book for 2022-23.

Dan Poynter's Legacy eBook Award

 globalebookawards.com

This award is for eBooks only. Winners are listed on the Global eBook Awards site. Authors pay a $79 entry fee per eBook per category.

The Writer's Digest Self-Published Book Award

 writersdigest.com

This is the only Writer's Digest competition exclusively for self-published books. Winners' names and book titles are published in the Writer's Digest, receive a subscription to the magazine, along with one year to the Writer's Digest Tutorials and 20% discount off of purchases made at Writer's Digest University.

The grand prize from eight categories is $10,000 in cash. Other prizes are $1,000 each.

Axiom Business Book Awards

 axiomawards.com

This business book awards platform is open to both traditional and self-published authors. They have a list of top named authors and are extremely well known in the business genre. The author entry fee is $75-$95.

The Eric Hoffer Book Award

 hofferaward.com

The Eric Hoffer Book Award entry fee is $55 with a grand prize of $2,500 awarded on an annual basis.

Next Generation Indie Book Awards

 indiebookawards.com

The Next Generation Indie Book Awards accepts entries of books in over eighty categories. Their awards are watched closely by publishers worldwide. Cash prizes range from $100 to $1,500 and the author entry fee is $75.

The International Best Indie Book Award

 bestindiebookaward.com

All entries into this awards program are accepted worldwide, must be written in English, and are limited to self and independently published authors. They are judged mostly on writing quality. The author entry fee is $50.

The IndieReader Discovery Awards

 indiereader.com

Judges for this book award program include the director of author and publishing relations at Amazon and two editors from Kirkus indie. Winners get announcement coverage in The Huffington Post, Wall Street Journal, and Publishers Weekly. The author entry fee is $150.

The National Book Critics Circle Award

 bookcritics

This annual book awards program judges in six categories, including fiction, nonfiction, biography, autobiography, poetry, and criticism. This awards program is considered very competitive and is highly recognized.

National Book Award by the National Book Foundation

 nationalbook.org

Winners in this book awards program receive a $10,000 prize and a bronze sculpture. Each finalist receives a prize of $1,000, a medal,

and a judge's citation. The author entry fee is $135 per title.

The Maxy Awards

 maxyawards.com

The annual grand prize winner receives $1,500 as an American Express Business Gift Card. One winner and one runner-up are selected and recognized in each genre category. Authors' entry fees are $65 for each category entered.

The Kirkus Prize

 kirkusreviews.com

This annual book award program has one of the richest literary awards in the world, with three prize winners of $50,000. Entries from authors of fiction, nonfiction, and young readers' literature are accepted on https://www.kirkusreviews.com/contests-giveaways/.

Andrew Carnegie Medal for Excellence in Nonfiction

 ala.org

The winner receives a $5,000 cash award, and two finalists in each category receive $1,500. There are no direct submissions to these awards—titles are drawn from the previous year's Booklist Editor's Choice: https://www.booklistonline.com/get-reviewed.

The Rubery Book Award

 ruberybookaward.com

This prestigious annual international book award program seeks the best books or eBooks by indie writers. All genres are accepted. The author's annual entry fee is currently $70.

Blue Ridge Mountains Christian Writers Conference, Contest/Book Awards

 blueridgeconference.com

This Christian book awards organization has three annual book contests: The Selahs, Directors' Choice, and Foundation Awards. The author entry fee is currently $45.

Living Now Book Awards

 livingnowawards.com

The awards are open to all books written in English (or bilingual). Every year, authors, publishers, and illustrators submit their titles until the awards close. After a judging period, gold, silver, and bronze medals are awarded in each category. The winning books are promoted on IndependentPublisher.com and to national media, and the medalists receive seals and medals to help market their award. The first early-bird entry fee is $75 per title, per category until a certain period and increases to $85 and $95 until the final deadline date.

Remember, book marketing and promotion seems like a lot when viewed as a whole, but clear, realistic, and measurable single steps, attentively followed, will tremendously increase the chance of success. There are many different strategies, but the preceding steps and avenues have been proven to produce excellent results for many book campaigns. Commitment to a Reasonable Strategies Task Schedule (RSTS) on a consistent basis produces increasing results.

"The journey of a thousand miles begins with . . . one step!" (Literary Devices, 2023) Take your first step toward riding the big wave of your book sales today. You're on your way.

The next chapter reveals a tried and true strategy to add another level of influence to your efforts to "get people talking." Let's discover the remarkable benefits of book club marketing.

CHAPTER

Book Club Marketing

The sales numbers are convincing. New authors who invest the time and effort to travel and present their book to local small book clubs and community organizations are more likely to start a marketing landslide of book sales. Marketing Landslide: an overwhelming, viral movement of buyer's attention that started with a small investment resulting in massive sales numbers.

Even if this is the digital age, and many aspects of effective marketing require online methods, when people meet an author in person they are much more likely to provide you with the most powerful marketing weapon in your arsenal: word-of-mouth advertising (WOMA). That's marketing landslide talk. That's why those two terms are synonymous: Book-Club-Marketing = WOMA.

If you aren't a gifted speaker simply let them know that you're a writer, not necessarily a speaker.

You don't have to be a dynamic speaker.

So, what do they need to hear from you? They need valuable, helpful content. And since you're the author, that means you're the authority. If you can present the valuable content of your book in a helpful way, they will love you.

Now, here's an extra powerful hint. Yes, this book club may be a small group of only 5-10 readers, but let them take a group picture with you (the famous author) for them to include on their website, Facebook page, or other advertising. Photos of you and your book are a powerful marketing tool.

For sure, those pictures will be texted and sent all over the area, to family members and friends, and picked up in more places than you can imagine. Who knows? You may see yourself in a Facebook snapshot you didn't expect.

dedicated to your audience topic is worth it. Your listing in these places will bring about more and more book sales that contribute to a marketing landslide.

Did you know there are paid book club marketing lists such as Buck Books (https://buckbooks.net)? They can reach tens of thousands of readers in a very short time. That depends on your budget, of course.

Book Launch (https://booklaunch.com) is also a great site to learn valuable information about launching your book, discovering the best book club lists, and how to use them to your benefit, producing more sales.

The idea here is to rub shoulders with as many community groups of people as possible, at least twice a month.

Let them get a picture standing next to you holding up your book.

One professional marketer recommended creating the "I've heard of you somewhere!" thing.

Another avenue of book club marketing is to get your book listed on Facebook Groups. It takes a focused effort and a little extra time, but searching diligently for other groups

Your name and face recognition in the community will contribute significantly to an increasing landslide of book sales.

A few important tips when attending community events is to show up with lots of business cards, after a good night's rest, books in the car, and lots of positive upbeat energy. The marketers say that these aspects are more than 50% of the battle in that setting.

Remember, speaking at book clubs and community organizations will seem like wasting valuable time compared to working diligently back home in the office online. The secret power of this strategy, though, is the chance to actually connect with your community in a personal, non-digital, real-person way. It can provide the most powerful marketing tool that can start a marketing landslide of sales.

Marketing landslides always seem very little to begin with. Give it time. It's true that Book-Club-Marketing = word-of-mouth-advertising (WOMA) = book sales.

TOP 10 Book Clubs - (can either be virtual, local, or both)

1. **Silent Book Club**
    silentbook.club

   Silent Book Club (SBC) is a global community of readers and introverts, with 300 chapters around the world led by local volunteers. SBC members gather in person and online to read together in quiet camaraderie. Silent Book Club is about community. Everyone is welcome, and anyone can join or launch a chapter.

   Their FB private group has 67.9K members

   https://www.facebook.com/groups/silentbookclub/

2. **New York Public Library and WNYC Book Club**
    nypl.org

   This online book club is run by the most widely read professionals on the planet: librarians. After wrapping up each month's read, enjoy watching a conversation with the book's author on the book club's website. That behind-the-scenes glimpse of authors' writing processes is what makes this book club extra special.

3. **Oprah's Book Club**
    oprah.com

   This standout was founded by Oprah Winfrey more than twenty-five years ago. The iconic entertainer and philanthropist is known for choosing thought-provoking books, many by female authors, that often go on to win awards or become bestsellers. Taking part in the reading community is as simple as reading each month's selection and subscribing to Oprah's Book Club Newsletter for reviews and discussion points.

4. Andrew Luck Book Club

 andrewluckbookclub.com

The mission of the Andrew Luck Book Club is to build a team of readers of all levels. It's very simple to participate; there is no sign up or log in. Just find a copy of the current book and start reading. After that go to AndrewLuckBookClub.com to see what others are posting about the book, and listen to the podcasts where he interviews selected authors. Feel free to post photos and thoughts about the books on Facebook, Instagram, and/or Twitter.

5. Now Read This

 pbs.org

The official online book club from PBS News Hour and The New York Times, Now Read This, selects a book each month, facilitates online book discussions, and then presents a Q&A session with the author.

6. The Reddit Book Club

 reddit.com

Most members read several books per month. All selections are chosen by popular vote after nominations from other members. But the beauty is in the simplicity: there are no membership requirements, and it's fine if you don't get around to reading all of the tomes. The Reddit Book Club keeps it simple with gently suggested reads and lively text-based discussions.

7. Books and Boba

 booksandboba.com

This is a book club and podcast dedicated to spotlighting books written by authors of Asian descent. Every month, hosts Marvin Yueh and Reera Yoo pick a book by an Asian or Asian American author to read and discuss on the podcast. In addition to book discussions, they also interview authors and cover publishing news, including book deals and new releases.

8. BookSparks Book Club

 booksparks.com

Through their online platform, the creators of BookSparks aim to "spark conversations about books and authors in fun, fresh ways." Along with a website that offers both blog posts and publication services for author clients, BookSparks moderates a string of book clubs throughout the year on their Instagram page.

9. PureWow Book Club

 purewow.com

PureWow Book Club focuses on reading and discussing one book each month. As the host of the book club changes each month, there is no set theme for the books selected.

10. The Social Book Club

 instagram.com/thesocialbookclub/

The Social Book Club enhances the experience of the traditional book club by catering to the growing online generation. Created by Lizzy Jensen, the Social Book Club selects culturally and historically relevant books for discussion each month. While there is no specific theme, it provides readers with a selection of inspiring reads from a variety of author perspectives. If you are interested in biographies, autobiographies, or touching fiction stories that connect the human race, The Social Book Club may be the perfect online network for you.

11. Book Clubs

 bookclubs.com/join-a-book-club/ local-in-person

This site contains different lists of local book clubs that are helpful if an author wants to connect to these local book clubs, depending upon where the author is located.

For certain, everyone is now clearly getting the core idea of good book marketing. A culmination of many different marketing strategies, applied consistently, causes a continual rise in exposure, familiarity with your message and book, and finally, sales, sales, sales.

By persistently employing more and more strategies one at a time, the days of anemic, sickly sales figures are over.

But wait. There's more. It's like one more amazing "kung fu" move added to an already great set of strategies for the champion to become unbeatable and awesome. This next chapter helps an independent author go from good . . . to great.

14

CHAPTER

Get Podcast Interviews & Features

Let me expose you to a match made in heaven waiting to happen: you need to expose your book AND most podcast hosts are looking for guests.

In the right scenario, you could offer podcast hosts a win-win. They get great content and you get the exposure you need. Are you ready?

One of the ULTIMATE beneficial methods to market your book that deserves special attention is to appear on podcast shows. You're an author now, so podcast appearances and reviews are an awesome way to build your authority and reach a bigger audience. Yes.

Podcast interviews help to sell more books, and they sometimes go viral almost overnight.

Each podcast interview becomes added proof of your book and expertise in your portfolio. Your portfolio includes a copy of your book, your expertise and background, other writings you have authored, and a list of podcasts and interviews you have conducted regarding your book. Any or all these items will be important in your marketing efforts going forward.

In order to get booked you will need to prepare:

1. Your portfolio

2. Your offer

3. Your vision

Prepare Your Portfolio

Your book is only one part of your portfolio. Within your book you likely have 3-4 keynote messages. If you're given twenty minutes to talk about something, what will it be? What's your passion? What makes your heart sing? What stories can you tell that will engage an audience?

Vulnerability sells.

In a public relations seminar by Jill Lublin (https://jilllublin.com/about-jill/), she told a very special story about a man blind from age seven. With great diligence and tenacity, he overcame his difficulty and became a successful financial expert. Then, after gathering a team, he was faced with the necessity of marketing strategies which seemed like another stone wall to overcome. Finally, with persistent encouragement, he allowed them to include in a press release that he had been "blind since seven." That was his point of vulnerability, difficult to share. Can you guess what happened? A reporter picked up on that little known fact, called him, and did an interview that was widely read. It went viral. Can you guess what happened to his sales?

When preparing for a podcast it is highly recommended to be personable, passionate about your subject, and vulnerable. That combination will make your podcast episode more memorable, and maybe even go viral. Can you imagine what that could do to your book sales?

Your portfolio should include:

1. A brief bio about yourself and your book.

2. 3-4 outlines of twenty minute talks you can give.

3. What points will you make?

4. What value will you offer to the audience?

5. Interview questions.

6. What will you give away?

Give it everything you've got. That means to find your uniqueness and exploit it boldly.

Your personal story and challenges are meant to be shared with the world.

Prepare Your Offer

Good podcast hosts are looking for content that will add value to their audience. Having a dud guest could bomb their show. Make sure to offer the hosts something that will add value to their audience.

This is not necessarily your book. Unless you're pitching to a book discussion podcast most hosts are not looking for people with a new book to come onto their show in order to sell their book. Your value add needs to be more than your book. If your book is about financial management and you can talk about preparing a budget then say:

> I'm an author of "Financial Management" and I'm looking for opportunities to help people prepare a budget.

You will get to the talk about your book but the episode will offer the audience more than the opportunity to buy your book. Think about it. When was the last time you subscribed to a podcast that every week only offered people another book to buy? Most people are not interested in those kinds of episodes. You must add value to every audience you address.

Don't forget generosity marketing we discussed in chapter three. Offering the host a few copies of your book to give away is a value add for their audience.

Make the host look like a rockstar and you'll go far. The more value you add to their audience the more willing they will be to help you sell your book.

Prepare Your Vision

What shows do you want to pitch to? If you're selling a children's book you might not want to be a guest on a crime show.

Where do we find podcast opportunities? Local colleges, local radio stations, and by conducting searches for local podcast hosts open to new interview opportunities are productive ways.

Don't forget to ask your interviewer if they can recommend to you another podcaster friend, as well. Podcasters are always diligently looking for interviews and helpful content for their viewers. It keeps their broadcasts alive. If you can show how your book is valuable to readers, the podcast community will get to know you very quickly and may be knocking on your door.

Before reaching out to a new podcast host, be sure to do some research to discover and understand their audience. It will be important for you to discuss with the host how your book uniquely connects with his or her followers. It is also good to research as much information about the host as possible to clearly know their podcast name, personal name or nickname, their expertise, the podcast's popularity numbers, and any other pertinent information. This will help communicate your professionalism and interest in him or her.

Prepare your offer and start emailing it out to podcast hosts for the shows where you'd like to appear. Follow-up every 3 days until you hear back from them. Some will book you right away. Some will book you for 6 months from now. If you work it you can be doing 3-4 podcast shows a month. Hit it hard for a week. Get some shows scheduled. Then dedicate a day a month to keep it going. You'll launch a podcast tour in no time.

My first book, *Audacious Generosity,* released in November 2020. I was an unknown author with a book to sell. The world was shut down because of the Covid-19 pandemic. Book signing tours were not possible. Instead, I appeared on over twenty podcast shows. It helped me expose my book, test my messages, and become a better speaker.

Finally, in the last short chapter, we present to you a powerful yet often overlooked strategy that has proven to bring independent book sales to peak. Let's talk about reaching out to influencers.

CHAPTER

Reach Out to Influencers

High profile people with special influence and recognition for your book's audience can provide a significant boost to your book promotions. Their endorsements provide strong social proof to your website, social media, advertising, podcasts, and every other aspect of effective marketing efforts.

If approached wisely, high profile influencers will love to help you because they have a business or connections with the same people your book speaks to. Your credibility gets a boost from their endorsement.

High profile influencers get increased popularity by recommending valuable help to their audience . . . you.

It's a win-win situation.

Identify the influencers in your niche, reach out to them, tell them who you are, and ask if they can help promote your latest book. Oftentimes, they will have a personal blog or YouTube review site where they will be glad to include you and your book for an episode.

Who are these influencers? Believe it or not, the traditional press and media may be interested in including you as a local author in their publications. In addition, look for social media influencers and bloggers within your subject area. Similar authors are often very open to a fellow writer's materials. Be sure to go for it and connect with national experts in the field of your study. They often are more open and easier to talk with than you might think. Finally, don't forget your own professional network. Your friends, family, and associates may have their own blogs, YouTube channels, and other ways to promote your book.

Reaching out to the right people to endorse and recommend you and your book helps insert you into the professional community, and this is an important part of marketing and sales.

Conclusion

Practice What You Preach

We've all heard the admonishment to practice what you preach. I can honestly say I've personally done that in this book. Every chapter and every tactic has been tested and proven to be effective. My team and I have implemented the research for our clients and every book we publish. These marketing tactics work.

Join our Team.

We are not done yet. While I stand behind the word ULTIMATE in the title, I'm sure there are other tactics to be added in the years to come. If you have proven success through a tactic that is not mentioned in this book, please email me at kevin@spiritmedia.us. Teach me. Let us learn from you. Who knows, you might get hired or at least receive a free gift card.

Some Authors Refuse to Market

Please don't settle for less. Most books sell fewer than 250 copies. They are put on the market but never marketed. At Spirit Media® we wholeheartedly believe that the message of God through the people of God is worthy to be taken to the nations.

> Psalm 96:3 (NLT) says, "Publish his glorious deeds among the nations. Tell everyone about the amazing things he does."

There are 195 nations of the world that need to receive God's message through you. Why not go for it? Where God guides He provides.

If God has called you to write, He has called you to market. Imagine a baker being called to bake. They mix cake batter but never put it into the oven. We'd shake our heads in disbelief. Actually, we should shake our heads in disbelief over any author who refuses to market their book.

I have no doubt this book can guide you to effectively market your book. Here's to your book sales!

Some Authors Hate to Market

If you agree that you need to market your book but like most authors hate marketing, then please consider allowing Spirit Media® to partner with you for all your publishing and marketing needs.

Spirit Media® can help you:

- Write your book

- Edit your book

- Publish your book

- Market your book

- Develop your brand

- Build your website

- Execute your marketing

- Take God's Message through you to the nations.

And, it is never too late or too early to let Spirit Media® makeover your book.

Our Authors Love Spirit Media

No one does more for you than Spirit Media®. Compare our prices and you'll find our prices are among the most competitive in the publishing and marketing industry.

Spirit Media® is reinventing publishing in three ways:

1. Connecting publishing and branding together.

2. Marketing before publishing.

3. Publishing in every format everywhere.

Let us know how we can serve you.

Stay in Touch

I'd love to hear from you. Email me at kevin@spiritmedia.us.

Reference List

1. **Haines, Derek.** 2021. "Why The Amazon Books Store Has A Monopoly On Book Sales."

   🌐 justpublishingadvice.com/why-do-amazon-sell-more-ebooks-than-other-retailers/

2. **Kirsch, Katrina.** 2022. "The Ultimate List of Email Marketing Stats for 2022." B2C Email Marketing Statistics. Posted November 30, 2022

   🌐 blog.hubspot.com/marketing/email-marketing-stats?hubs_content=blog.hubspot.com

3. **Literary Devices.** 2023. "A Journey of a Thousand Miles Begins with a Single Step."

   🌐 literarydevices.net/a-journey-of-a-thousand-miles-begins-with-a-single-step/

4. **Oberlo.** 2023. "TikTok Users by Age."

   🌐 oberlo.com/statistics/tiktok-age-demographics

5. **Sinek, Simon. n.d.** "Start with Why." Accessed January 17, 2023.

   🌐 simonsinek.com/books/start-with-why/

6. **World Population Review.** 2023. "Time Spent Reading (2017-2022)."

   🌐 worldpopulationreview.com/country-rankings/average-books-read-per-year-by-country

7. **Zhou, Luiza.** 2023. "Email Marketing ROI Statistics: The Ultimate List in 2023." Updated: January 7, 2023.

   🌐 luisazhou.com/blog/email-marketing-roi-statistics/

Made in the USA
Columbia, SC
07 April 2023

14522657R00074